A KEY TO COMMON ALGAE

Freshwater, Estuarine and some Coastal Species

E.G. Bellinger *PhD, FIWEM, FRSA*

Fourth Edition

The Institution of Water and Environmental Management

©The Institution of Water and Environmental Management 1992
ISBN 1 870752 16 3

First published as 'A Key to the Identification of the More Common Algae Found in Water Undertakings in Britain'. *Journal of the Society of Water Treatment and Examination*, 1969, **18**, 2.

Second edition published as 'A Key to the Identification of the More Common Algae Found in British Freshwaters'. *Ibid*, 1974, **23**, 1.

Third edition published separately by The Institution of Water Engineers and Scientists as 'A Key to Common British Algae' 1980.

The Institution of Water and Environmental Management
15 John Street, London WC1N 2EB

PREFACE

For many years algae have caused a range of problems such as red tides, fish kills and blocked filters. Their removal, in order to provide wholesome potable water, has been a continuing economic burden. With increasing demands for water worldwide, engineers have had to utilize sources with lower water quality and often increased algal problems. A good knowledge of these algae is an essential pre-requisite to successful treatment and control whatever the situation.

Although the majority of freshwater, estuarine and coastal water algae (non attached) are small (i.e. miscroscopic), they are very diverse in their structure and requirements. Whilst I was working in the water industry these differences were brought home to me by the variety of problems caused by the different species. This emphasised the need to identify the algae present in order to make sensible decisions to overcome these problems, and to understand their ecology in order to manage water bodies in the future.

The book is not intended as a comprehensive review of the algae. It does not aim to deal with their physiology or ecology nor does it intend to explore their detailed taxonomy for I feel that such detail is not generally required by practitioners in the water industry or general ecologists. If such information is required, several excellent and detailed texts are available (see bibliography). This text is meant to be a guide to the identification of the more commonly encountered species – it is a key and is thus not in taxonomic order.

As the fourth in a series of keys started in 1969 in response to requests by waterworks biologists, it has been expanded and revised and now includes some estuarine and coastal water species, as well as freshwater lake and riverine ones. The identification features used are mainly morphological and require nothing more than a good light microscope to see. This approach is deliberate as I feel that most workers will not have sophisticated techniques (such as electron microscopy) available in their laboratories. It is meant to be a bench tool and as such its usefulness can only be assessed by user feedback, so comments are always welcome.

My hope is that the key will help people to name and thus understand the algae present in their waters, and that it will in turn provide a rational basis for treatment, control and management where required.

E.G. BELLINGER
March 1992

iii

CONTENTS

1. INTRODUCTION

Microalgae comprise a very diverse group of plants. They occur all over this planet being found in habitats as varied as damp soil, tree trunks, rivers, lakes, rocky sea shores, open seas, effluents from hot springs and snow.

Most are microscopic in size but many occur in groups or colonies which are large enough to see with the naked eye. Observation on the detailed structure of individual cells still requires either light or electron microscopy however. A few species do have individual cells large enough to see with the naked eye, e.g. *Nitella*. In its broadest sense the term algae describes all holophytic organisms (as well as their numerous colourless derivatives) that fail to reach the highest level of differentiation characteristic of the archegoniate plants.[1] To delineate the algae, more detailed studies on such things as life histories, internal cell structure and biochemistry, than are appropriate to this work are required. Such detail can be obtained from the texts listed in the bibliography. For the purposes of this key algae in five divisions (according to Lee[2]) are described. These are the Cyanophyta, Chromophyta, Rhodophyta, Chlorophyta and Charophyta. Within the Chromophyta seven classes are included.

For an outline of algal taxonomy readers are referred to Round[3] and for more detailed work to Christiansen.[4] It is, however, necessary to understand the suffixes normally used in algal taxonomy and the names given to the various levels of organisation. The endings normally used are:

Class .... phyceae
Order .... ales
Family .... aceae
Genus ....usually a Greek or Latin name
Species ....usually a Latin name
Variety ....usually a Latin name

The algae reported in this key are not in taxonomic order. The purpose of the key is to aid identification. The division and class of each species is recorded in the index. In general the features used for identification are morphological. On many occasions, however, certain features of internal cell structure and biochemistry may also be needed. An outline of the main features of interest is given overleaf.

2. GENERAL MORPHOLOGICAL FEATURES

2.1. General shape

The shape of algae varies from simple non-motile single cells to multicellular three dimensional structures. For the purposes of this key, with the exception of *Chara*, *Nitella* and *Enteromorpha*, the shapes are relatively simple and are illustrated in Figure 1. The simplest shape is that of the unicell which may be either motile or non-motile (Figs. 1a, b, c). Colonial versions of both motile and non-motile forms exist and represent a greater degree of complexity (Figs. 1d, e, f, g). Filamentous types may be either unbranched (1h) or branched (1i). Two types of colony are known. In some forms there is an indefinite number of cells and the colony continues to grow by individual cells dividing. The colony reproduces by fragmentation. In others there is a fixed number of cells from the start and no new cells are produced for that colony during its life. This is called a coenobium. It should be noted that parallel series of development occur in different classes of algae. For example non-motile gelatinous palmelloid colonies occur in the Chlorophyceae, Xanthophyceae and Chrysophyceae (although the latter two are less common) and filamentous types occur in the Chlorophyceae, Cyanophyceae, Xanthophycaea, Bacillariophyceae and some others.

Cell structure and shape within the diatoms (Bacillariophyceae) is a little more complex and important from the point of view of identification. Our understanding of the structure of the diatom frustule (the silica impregnated box like structure surrounding the cell) has increased markedly with the advent of the electron microscopy.

The frustule is made of silica and is composed of two, almost equal, overlapping halves (Fig. 2) fitting together somewhat like a petri dish. The large half if the epitheca, the smaller the hypotheca. Each half has a more or less flat surface – the valve surface – and an edge area – the connecting band. The two connecting bands, one from each theca, comprise the girdle. There may be additional bands between the valve and the girdle called the girdle bands or intercalary bands. Where the valve surface bends towards the girdle the area is called the mantle. Because the silica is deposited in a regular way characteristic regular ornamentation develops on the frustule. Hendey[5] recognised four basic patterns in ornamentation; centric (e.g. *Cyclotella)*, Trellisoid (e.g. *Eunotia*), Gonoid (e.g. *Triceratium*) and Pennate (e.g. *Navicula*). From the point of view of general identification, however, it is more common to recognise two basic shapes, centric and pennate. Centric diatoms usually have valves which are circular in outline with markings arranged symmetrically around a central point. Pennate diatoms are usually elongate or linear with their markings arranged transversely to the long axis. Some pennate diatoms have a raphe system, the raphe being a longitudinal slot in the theca (Fig. 2). This is divided into two parts,

2

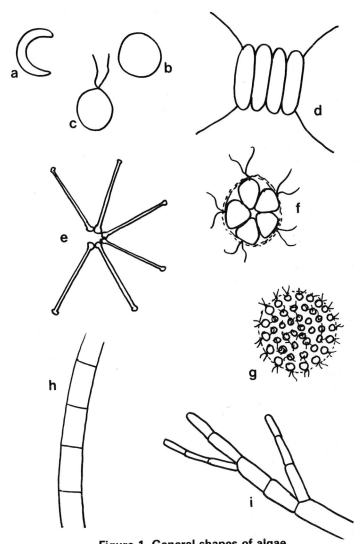

Figure 1. General shapes of algae
Non-motile unicells: (a) Selenastrum (b) Chlorella. **Motile unicell:**
(c) Chlamydomonas. **Non-motile colony:** (d) Scendesmus
(e) Asterionella. **Motile colony:** (f) Pandorina (g) Volvox.
Unbranched filament (h). **Branched filament** (i).

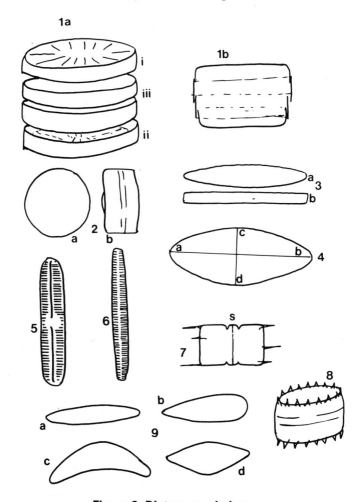

Figure 2. Diatom mophology
1.(a) & (b) components of the frustule; (i) epivalve, (ii) hypovalve,
(iii) girdle bands. 2. centric diatom; (a) valve view, (b) girdle view.
3. pennate diatom; (a) valve view, (b) girdle view. 4. planes of
symmetry; a-b = apical axis, c-d = transapical axis. 5. pennate
diatom with raphe. 6. with pseudoraphe. 7. Sulcus (s) on a
Melosira. 8. spines on margin of Stephanodiscus. 9. valve shapes;
(a) isopolar, (b) heteropolar, (c) asymmetrical, (d) symmetrical.

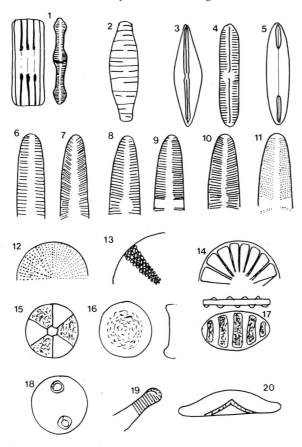

Figure 3. Diatom valve markings
1. internal septa. 2. transapical costae. 3. raphe in thickened ribs.
4. normal raphe. 5. shortened raphe in ribs. 6. parallel striae.
7. radiate striae. 8. central area round. 9. central area transverse.
10. central area small. 11. central area acute angled stauros.
12. punctae in radial rows interspersed with subradial rows.
13. coarse areolae. 14. areolae grouped in segments. 15. sections
of valve face alternately raised and depressed giving shaded
appearance. 16. central region raised or depressed. 17. pennate
with raised or depressed areas. 18. ocelli on surface.
19. rudimentary raphe as in Eunotia. 20. raphe curved to point at
centre as in Epithemia.

each part starting from the central nodule and terminating with a polar nodule. Other pennate diatoms have a clear unornamented area, running down the centre of the valve but this contains no sot through the theca and is called a pseudoraphe. Some species have a pseudoraphe, some a pseudoraphe on one valve and a true raphe on the other and yet others a true raphe on each valve. The planes of symmetry and the axes are shown in Figure 2. A full description of the markings and structures on the frustule can be found in Barber and Haworth[6] or Round et al.[7] but some of the more important ones are illustrated in Figure 3.

2.2 Cell wall

Most of the algae listed in this key have a definite cell wall. Some, e.g. *Gymnodinium* and *Pyramimonas*, have the protoplast enclosed by a membrane only. The main organic constituents of the cell walls are carbohydrates although lipids and proteins may be present. Cellulose walls predominate except in the Chrysophyceae and Bacillariophyceae where there is a marked tendency for silica deposition. Cell walls of the Cyanophyceae are similar to those of bacteria.

2.3 Photosynthetic pigments

Colour can be a useful indicator to the division to which an alga does or does not belong. This feature must be treated with some caution, however, as pigmentation can vary depending upon, for example, phase of growth[8] (*Botryococcus braunii* in culture appears green in the exponential growth phase but red in the stationary phase), staining of mucus surrounds masking the true cell-colour, or merely changing environmental conditions. For detailed and accurate assessment of photosynthetic pigments chemical analysis is needed. Three types of photosynthetic pigments are present. These are (a) chlorophylls, (b) carotenoids and, (c) biloproteins. Their distribution through the various divisions is given in Table I. The following points are of interest: first, chlorophyll-a is present in all algae, hence its use in biomass determinations; second, many of the carotenes and xanthophylls are characteristic of one or two divisions of algae and can thus be important diagnostic features; third, biloproteins are water soluble unlike the chlorophylls and carotenoids, which are lipid soluble; fourth, the proportions of one pigment to another varies from one division to another and it is these proportions which give many algae a characteristic colour e.g:

Chlorophyll-a dominant: green as in the Chlorophyceae and Euglenophyceae:

Carotenoids dominant: yellow-brown, yellow-golden or yellow-green in the Chrysophyceae, Dinophyceae, Cryptophyceae, Bacillariophyceae

Table I Distribution of the Main Pigments in Algae (taken from refs. 9 and 10, p 127)

	Cyanobacteria	Chlorophyceae	Xanthophyceae	Chrysophyceae	Bacillariophyceae	Pyrrophyceae	Cryptophyceae	Euglenophyceae
Chlorophylls								
Chlorophyll-a	+	+	+	+	+	+	+	+
Chlorophyll-b	−	+	−	−	−	−	−	+
Chlorophyll-c	−	−	−	?	+	+	+	−
Chlorophyll-d	−	−	−	?	−	−	−	−
Chlorophyll-e	−	−	+	−	−	−	−	−
Carotenoids								
Carotenes								
α-carotene	−	+	−	−	−	−	+	−
β-carotene	+	+	+	+	+	+	−	+
γ-carotene	−	+	−	−	−	−	−	−
Lycopene	−	+	−	−	−	−	−	−
ε-carotene	−	−	−	−	+	−	+	−
Xanthophylls								
lutein	+?	+	−	+?	−	−	−	−
violaxanthin	−	+	+?	−	−	−	−	−
fucoxanthin	−	−	−	+	+	−	−	−
neoxanthin	−	+	+?	−	−	−	−	+
astaxanthin	−	+	−	−	−	−	−	+
diatoxanthin	−	−	−	+	+	−	−	−
diadinoxanthin	−	−	−	+	+	+	−	−
zeaxanthin	+	+	−	−	−	−	+?	−
peridinin	−	−	−	−	−	+	−	−
dinoxanthin	−	−	−	−	−	+	−	−
antheroxanthin	−	−	−	−	−	−	−	+
myxoxanthin	+	−	−	−	−	−	−	−
myxoxanthophyll	+	−	−	−	−	−	−	−
oscilloxanthin	+	−	−	−	−	−	−	−
echinenone	+	−	−	−	−	−	−	−
Biloproteins								
C-phycocyanin ⎫ C-phycoerythrin ⎭	+	−	−	−	−	−	−	−
Phycocyanin ⎫ Phycoerythrin ⎭	−	−	−	−	−	−	+	−

and the Xanthophyceae: Biloproteins dominant: blue green as in the Cyanophyceae

2.4 Storage products

As a result of photosynthesis algae may produce more organic matter than is immediately required. The extra material may then be stored as a food reserve. The nature of this food reserve may vary from one algal class to another (see Table II). Starch is only found in the Chlorophyceae, Dinophyceae and Cryptophyceae. Starch may be easily detected as it will stain blue-black with iodine solution. Paramylum in the Euglenophyceae and leucosin in the Chrysophyceae and Bacillariophyceae are two other stored polysaccharides. Blue-green algae accumulate glycogen and glycoproteins. Oil and/or fats are stored by the Bacillariophyceae, Xanthophyceae, Chrysophyceae, Dinophyceae and Euglenophyceae.

The pyrenoid is a specialized proteinaceous region within the chloroplast that takes the products of photosynthesis and converts them into storage products. Pyrenoids do not occur in the blue-green algae but occur in all other classes.

2.5 Flagella

Flagella are found in all divisions of algae, with the exception of the Cyanophyta and Rhodophyta. For the purpose of the species listed in this key, however, flagella will not be found in the Xanthophyceae or Bacillariophyceae either (see Table II). Flagella vary in number, when present, from one to eight, and in their location from anterior to around the girdle. It should be noted that the delicacy of flagella frequently causes them to be shed in preserved samples, hence it is essential to identify from living specimens and to use a suitable preservative for other samples.

2.6 Other cell components

Recognition of many structures within an algal cell requires a good microscope and experience. The blue-green algae are termed Procaryotic, having no true nucleus bounded by a membrane. The other algae are termed Eucaryotic as they have a nucleus with membrane. The procaryotic algae are primitive in other respects as well. From the point of view of identification the most important of these is the fact that their photosynthetic pigments are not isolated into chloroplasts or chromotophores. The photosynthetic pigments appear to be evenly dispersed throughout the cell. Cells of blue-green algae do not always appear evenly coloured, however, as they may contain gas vacuoles (which often appear dark) and granules of stored food (usually

8

Table II Cytological Characteristics of the Main Classes of Freshwater Algae

	Nucleus	Chromatophores	Flagella	Storage products	Cell wall
Procaryota					
Cyanobacteria	—	—	—	glycogen and glycoprotein	indistinct, of cellulose or pectin
Eucaryota					
Chlorophyceae	+	+ grass green	± (2,4)	starch, pyrenoid sometimes present	cellulose
Euglenophyceae	+	+ green	+ (1, 2 or 3)	paramylum and oil	no true wall but pellicle which may be flexible
Xanthophyceae	+	+ yellow green	± (2)	oils and fats	present or absent, when present usually pectic and may be siliceous
Chrysophyceae	+	+ brownish	± (1 or 2)	oil and leucosin	no cellulose wall, membrane may be siliceous with scales
Bacillariophyceae	+	+ brownish green	—	oils and fats	strongly silicified in two halves with characteristic structures and often markings
Pyrrophyceae	+	+ greeny golden to brown	+ (2)	starch or oil	with or without cellulose wall, when present may be sculptured
Cryptophyceae	+	+ greeny brown	+ (2)	starch	mostly naked

Notes: + indicates presence; — indicates absence; numbers in brackets are commonest numbers present

Cyanophycin granules). It should also be noted that the cells of some eucaryotic algae, e.g. *Cladophora* and *Ankistrodesmus*, may have chloroplasts which fill the cell giving an even colouration. This can mislead an inexperienced observer into assuming there are no distinct chloroplasts, but other features such as colour or storage products will show that these are not blue-green algae.

3. SAMPLE PREPARATION AND PRESERVATION

For identification of algae it is essential to look at fresh living cells and only supplement these observations with preserved material. Thus, on each sampling occasion, whilst some material will be preserved for counting, etc., an aliquot should be kept live and fresh if possible and looked at immediately on return to the laboratory.

The numbers of algal cells may be so low that some form of concentration is necessary for easy observation. This may be achieved by collecting the fresh sample with a phytoplankton net. This does have the disadvantage that smaller species may be lost as they pass straight through the net meshes. Centrifugation or gentle filtration and resuspension can also be used but great care must be taken not to damage delicate species (especially flagellates). For samples which cannot be looked at quickly and must be preserved Lugol's iodine acidified with glacial acetic acid is recommended (150 gms KI, 50 gms I$_2$, 1,000cc distilled water and 20cc glacial acetic acid – use 2–3 mls./100 ml sample). As the iodine weights, as well as fixes, the cells this aids sedimentation which can be used for concentrating the cells. A 1:10 concentration can be achieved by placing 100cc of iodine fixed sample in a measuring cylinder and storing in a darkened area at an even temperature. Allow about one hour per cm depth of sample for sedimentation. During this period the algae will settle to the bottom. Carefully siphon off the top 90cc of supernatant liquid leaving the concentrated sample in the remaining 10cc. This works well for most algae, the exceptions being buoyant blue-greens. These can be made to settle by dispersing their gas vacuoles. This is done by placing the sample in a soft-walled polythene bottle so that it is completely full. The cap is screwed on tightly, and the bottle is dropped on to a hard surface from about 1½m. The sudden pressure-increase, as the bottle strikes the surface, collapses the vacuoles, allowing the algae to be sedimented.

Difficulty is sometimes experienced in determining whether there is a silica or cellulose wall present and, if the wall is silica, observing any patterning which might be present. If the sample is treated to remove organic matter and then examined for cell walls, if any have resisted the treatment they are probably silica. Removal of organic matter can be achieved as follows:

1. Place a drop of concentrated (preferably fresh) sample on a microscope slide.
2. Warm gently over alcohol flame or hot plate to dry film to slide.
3. Hold momentarily in flame to combust organic matter. If the algae are strongly silicified a further stage may be used.
4. Place two drops concentrated sulphuric acid on the film and warm gently. Evaporate the acid and gently wash the slide with distilled water. Any cleaned frustules can then be observed under a microscope.

The foregoing technique is adapted from Hendey[5]

For a more detailed cleaning technique the reader is advised to consult Hendey, also Lund.[11] For observations of wall markings it is necessary to mount the cleaned frustules in a high refractive index medium such as Hyrax, Naphrax, Pleurax or Piperine/antimony tribromide. (For more detail, see references 5 and 11.)

If fixation or preservation is necessary either because of the time interval required between collecting and observing or because there are fast moving flagellates present which are hard to observe whilst on the move the following may be used. The best general preservative is Lugal's iodine (see above). This does, however, impart a golden brown colour to the algae as well as staining any starch or blue-black colour. Gluteraldehyde solution (1%) can also be used which is colourless and hence does not stain the algae nor does it stain starch. It can also be dangerous to use and care should be taken to avoid contact with skin or inhalation. It is essential to wear rubber gloves.

4. A GUIDE TO MORE COMMON LAKE, RIVER AND SOME ESTUARINE ALGAE WITH SOME NOTES ON THEIR SIGNIFICANCE

Because of the diversity of species of freshwater algae detailed identification can often only be achieved by reference to specialised texts some of which may not be readily available. The more general identification keys available, which concentrate on common species, can prove difficult to use because they rely on the observers ability to distinguish between the main classes. Such an approach can lead to difficulties e.g. whether or not chloroplasts are present, whether flagella are present or is the cell wall silicified or not? Some of these difficulties arise because one is confronted with a preserved specimen. Whilst one is always recommended to identify primarily from fresh living material, if the samples are collected remote from the laboratory or, for example, samples are collected as a routine by other members of an organisation such as a water authority, preserved material is all one has and one has to make the best of it!

In order to try to overcome these problems I have used a two pronged approach. Firstly, there is a brief key to the main classes together with a table summarising their main features. Secondly, there is a longer dichotomising key based, where possible, on easily observable morphological characteristics together with some features revealed by simple staining techniques to identify to genera and species level. It should be noted, however, that even when using the second approach to identify to genera or species level a knowledge of the suspected class for that alga is of benefit as, although based primarily on morphology, organisms of the same class tend to be grouped within each morphological type.

4.1 Key to main classes

1. (a)   Cells having chloroplasts **2**
   (b)   Cells without chloroplasts, pigment evenly dispersed throughout the cell (although presence of food granules and gas vacuoles may give appearance of cell pigments being divided up). Pigmentation usually blue-green, olive, red or brownish. Where sheaths present they may be coloured. Cell walls, especially cross walls, thin and in some species not at all obvious. No flagellated forms present .... **Cyanobacteria**

2. (a)   Chloroplasts either strong or pale grass green **3**
   (b)   Chloroplasts golden, brown, yellowish, red, blue or some other colour **6**

3. (a)   Storage product starch as indicated by iodine-starch test* **4**
   (b)   storage product not starch-iodine test negative **5**

4. (a)   Plants macroscopic, large erect upto and greater than 400mm in height, branched with branches arranged in whorls. Cells large each containing numerous chloroplasts .... **Charophyceae**
   (b)   Plants microscopic (except when in large masses or strands), unicellular colonial or filaments. One or 2 but sometimes many chloroplasts. May have flagella, usually 2 (rarely 4) at anterior end of equal length. Starch +ve .. .. **Chlorophyceae**

---

* It should be noted that the amount of starch present depends upon the physiological state of the cell and, even when present, in very small cells it may not give a very strong +ve test.

5. (a)   Unicells with single emergant flagellum (stout in structure) at apical end. Two to many chloroplasts. Storage product paramylum. Cell wall may be elastic or metabolic, i.e. it can change shape .... **Euglenophyceae**

   (b)   Unicells, colonies or filaments. Two or more disc shaped chloroplasts per cell. If flagella present 2 per cell one markedly longer than other .... **Xanthophyceae**

6. (a)   Cells with 2 flagella not emerging from apex but from central region. One passes round the cell in a central furrow the other passes downwards along its longitudinal axis. Cell wall smooth or covered with plates. Cells solitary either roughly spherical or with projecting horns. Numerous disc shaped chloroplasts usually brownish in colour but may be yellow or even reddish or blueish. May give starch +ve test .... **Dinophyceae**

   (b)   Cells not as above **7**

7. (a)   Cells with a rigid cell wall impregnated with silica (often heavily) and usually ornamented. (Cells may need cleaning to observe ornamentation in some cases – see page 10.) Cell wall made up of two overlapping halves. Overall shape often different in different views (see intro p. 2) but generally round, needle shaped, cigar shaped or crescent shaped in one view. Often isolated but can form colonies, filaments or ribbons. No flagella but some may perform gliding movements. One to many chloroplasts golden brown to brown in colour .... **Bacillariophyceae**

   (b)   Cells without silica wall, not as above **8**

8. (a)   Cells with no flagella or if flagella present either one long one or one long and one quite short **9**

   (b)   Cells with two flagella of approximately equal length (only slightly unequal) which arise from a small depression at the anterior end. Chloroplasts 2 or 1. Usually olive green or slightly golden but can be reddish or blueish. Starch test +ve .... **Cryptophyceae**

9. (a)   Plants with encrusting often complex filamentous structure – rarely solitary. One to many chloroplasts per cell. Olive green, or can be reddish or blueish. Starch test +ve. No flagella .... **Rhodophyceae**

   (b)   Cells solitary or colonial sometimes simple filaments. Flagella may be present (one single or one long one short). Chloroplasts yellow to brown 1–2 per cell. Starch test −ve. .... **Chrysophyceae**

4.2 Key to main genera and species

1. (a)   Plants macroscopic, erect in habit with branches arranged in whorls along main axis. May be up to and even greater than 400mm in height. .... **Charophyceae 2**

    (b)   Plants microscopic or if visible to the naked eye as a mass or group requiring a microscope to determine their general morphology **3**

2. (a)   Plants coarse to touch frequently encrusted with lime (common name Stonewort) .... **Chara**   **Chara** thrives in hard still or slow flowing waters. Species of this genus noted for their characteristic odour like garlic. (I.1)

    (b)   Plants not coarse to touch, deep green in colour, not encrusted with lime .... **Nitella**   **Nitella** has no rough coating as in **Chara** and prefers soft waters. May impart a septic or garlic odour to the water. (I.2)

3. (a)   Cells grouped together to form a filament, strand or ribbon (see glossary for all three terms) frequently large enough, en masse, to see with the naked eye **4**

    (b)   Cells isolated or in regular or irregular groups but *not* forming a filament, strand or ribbon. **54**

4. (a)   Cell pigments localized in chloroplasts pale green, deep grass green, golden to brown, olive rarely blueish or reddish **5**

    (b)   Cell pigments not localized in chloroplasts blue-green, olive or red-brown colour (see note in glossary for help with these features). **42**

5. (a)   Filaments branched (sometimes one needs to look at several filaments and along a reasonable length to detect branching) **6**

    (b)   Filaments or ribbons unbranched **24**

6. (a)   Branches of filaments rejoin to form a net   **Hydrodictyon**   **Hydrodictyon** is a member of the Chlorophyceae. Commonly known as the water net it can form dense growths in lakes, ponds, rivers, ditches and shallow waters. It often prefers hard waters and also those which are nutrient rich. Cells large and multinucleate, cylindrical in shape attached to each other at their ends. Meshes of net usually of 5–6 cells, each cell forming one side. Chloroplasts reticulate with many pyrenoids. Only one British species .... **H.reticulatum** (Plate I.3)

    (b)   branches of filaments do not rejoin to form a net **7**

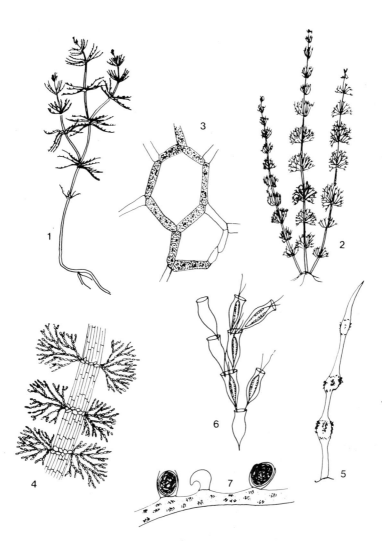

Plate I. 1. Chara. 2. Nitella. 3. Hydrodictyon reticulatum. 4. Batrachospermum. 5. Lemanea. 6. Dinobryon. 7. Vaucheria.

7. (a)   Each cell in a flask-shaped lorica open at one end, one or two loricas arising from the mouth of another forming a forked or dendroid series (see glossary and Plate I Fig. 6 for fuller explanation) .... **Dinobryon**
Dinobryon usually forms free swimming dendroid colonies which may contain up to 50 cells. The lorica is usually clear but can sometimes be stained with iron. Cells are elongated oval with a short contractile stalk at lower end attaching to the lorica (may be difficult to see) Cells 3–5μm br 20–60μm l. Loricas up to 70μm long. Food reserve leucosin. A planktonic species in lakes and rivers can be abundant in oligo/mesotrophic waters but can occur where there is more enrichment as well. Commonly produces a spherical cyst within each lorica at certain times of the year (cysts 10–15μm br). May impart a noxious taste or odour to the water. Member of the Chrysophyceae, the most common species is **D.divergens** – other species can be difficult to separate. (Plate I.6).

(b)   Cells not in flask-shaped loricas **8**

8. (a)   Filaments siphonaceous (no cross walls), irregularly branched, cross walls only occur when reproductive structures are produced .... **Vaucharia**
Vaucheria filaments are often inter-woven to form mats in shallower water or on damp mud. Branching is irregular and cross walls absent except where reproductive structures are formed. Numerous disc shaped chloroplasts. No pyrenoids. Oil droplets may be present. For full description of reproduction see (1). More than 50 freshwater species have been described based mainly on reproductive organ structure. Filaments, which can be up to 220μm broad, are often found in harder waters at colder times of the year. (Plate I.7).

(b)   Filaments with normal cross walls not siphonaceous **9**

9. (a)   Filaments multiseriate i.e. cells in many parallel or radiating rows, may or may not have branches. **10**

(b)   Filaments not multiseriate **12**

10. (a)   Filaments branched although not always clearly so. ... **11**

(b)   Filaments unbranched **12**

11. (a)   Plant with filaments loosely arranged and embedded in copious mucilage. Main branch multiaxial with regular tufts of branches (which are uniaxial)   **Batrachospermum**
Plants consist of a main axis which is multilayered. Tufts of branches arise at regular intervals and are composed of barrel shaped cells (uniaxial) commonly known as frog-spawn because of its large amounts of mucilage. Usually

	an olive green/brown or even greyish colour. Found in clean flowing waters in shady position. **Batrachospermum** is a member of the Rhodophyceae (Plate I.4).
11. (b)	Plant without regular tufts of branches, bristle like rarely bushy habit, with a series of thickened areas along stem . ... **Lemanea** Plant consisting of a simple or branched bristle like structure with regular swellings. Occurs in flowing water in upland areas. **Lamanea** is a member of the Rhodophyceae (Plate I.5).
12. (a)	Cells stacked in vertical rows growing over stones in red or brown masses .... **Hildenbrandia** The thalli of **Hildenbrandia** grow over stones, in hard water, and consist of tiers of cells packed side by side (giving appearance of closely packed loosely arranged filaments). Cells 7–12μm long but thalli can be up to 10μm diameter and 200μm thick. Chloroplasts numerous, frequent pyrenoids, starch +ve usualy gives dark brown colour). (Plate II.1)
(b)	Filaments attached; radiate from central point forming flattened disc or slightly rounded cushion of cells some of which have fine hairs or setae which are sheathed at the base. .... **Coleochaetae** **Coleochaetae**, a member of the Chlorophyceae, grows as a flat disc or cushion on rocks or plants. Some cells have setae sheathed at their bases which arise through special pores or blepharoplasts. Cells up to 40μm long, disc up to 1mm in diameter. Chloroplasts parietal with a pyrenoid. (Plate II.2).
13. (a)	At least some cells of filament bearing setae or hairs . **14**
(b)	No setae present **18**
14. (a)	Setae having a bulbous base **15**
(b)	Setae without bulbous base **16**
15. (a)	Filaments growing horizontally or prostrate, epiphytic. Branching irregular may be absent. Some cells with one to several hairs. .... **Aphanochaetae** **Aphanochaetae** is a prostrate creeping epiphyte but, being small, can often be missed. Cells cylindrical bearing one or more setae, per cell, with bulbous bases. Cells 6 to 15μm broad with parietal chloroplasts and 1–2 pyrenoids. Plate II.3). Chlorophyceae.
(b)	Filaments not prostrate, unilaterally branched, somewhat broader at top than the base. Most terminal cells have one or more chaetae with swollen base arising from end

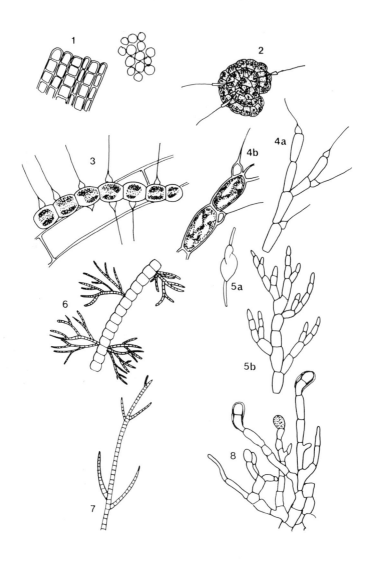

Plate II. 1. Hildenbrandia. 2. Coleochaetae. 3. Aphanochaetae. 4. Bulbochaetae. 5. Chaetophora. 6. Draparnaldia. 7. Stigeoclonium. 8. Gongrosira.

of cell. .... **Bulbochaetae**
Bulbochaetae has branched filaments and is easily identified
by the setae with distinctly swollen bases. Cells slightly
barrel shaped and a little wider at top than bottom 10–
35br and 2–4 long as broad. Oogonia sometimes develop
terminally or lateraly. Chloroplast reticulate, parietal with
pyrenoids. In slow flowing or still, particularly hard,
waters. (Plate II.4). Chlorophyceae.

16. (a)   Filaments enclosed in soft watery mucilage which has no
definite shape **17**

   (b)   Mucilage firm, definite shape, forming macroscopic
attached masses .... **Chaetophora**
Chaetophora filaments are attached to stones or aquatic
plants. They are highly branched and these branches
taper to a rounded end or a long tapering multicelullar
hair which may project beyond the firm mucilage which
encloses the filaments. Chloroplasts parietal or band like;
1 or more pyrenoids per cell. Cells 4–15μm broad, up to
$\times$ 10 as long as broad. **Chaetophora** occurs attached at
the margins of lakes or ponds. In hard waters plants can
become calcified. (Plate II.5). Chlorophyceae.

17. (a)   Filament axis composed of large cells from which arise
tufts of branches composed of much smaller cells ....
.... **Draparnaldia**
Draparnaldia characterised by the marked difference in
size between the main axis cells and the branches. Axis
cells barrel-shaped (sometimes cylindrical) 20–130μm
wide. Branch cells only 5–10μm broad. Branches alternate,
opposite or whorled. Branches terminate in rounded cells
or setiforous cells. Chloroplasts parietal, net like or
banded, 1 or more pyrenoids. The whole plant has a
feathery appearance and forms large (1–10cm) bright
green tufts attached to stones or other objects. More
common in cooler, cleaner slower flowing waters. (Plate
II.6). Chlorophyceae.

   (b)   Filament main axis cells not markedly different from
branch cells .... **Stigeoclonium**
Filaments of **Stigeoclonium** are usually attached by means
of basal cells which may develop into an extensive disc.
Filament cells 8–25μm broad with cells 2 to 5 $\times$ lab.
Chloroplasts parietal, pyrenoid present. Branches may
arise regularly or irregularly and usually taper to form a
fine hair or point, the tapering involving more than one
cell. Common epiphytic species in shallow
polluted/enriched waters.

19

The two commonest species are **S.tenue** in which the main filament cells < 14µm in diameter, cells longer more delicate. **S.lubricum** has longer main filament cells > 14µm which are more robust and barrel shaped. Both species are extensively branched. (Plate II.7). Chlorophyceae.

18. (a) Branched filaments embedded in mucilage **19**
    (b) Branched filaments not with mucilage **21**
19. (a) Plant forming gelatinous globular cushions. Mucilage may be tough and could be encrusted with lime **20**
    (b) Mucilage covering thin; plants of upright trailing branched filaments arising from basal attachment cells (may be disc). Not cushion like or globular **Sigeoclonium (see 17)**
20. (a) Cushions composed of filaments with finely tapering apices with either rounded end cell or long tapering multicellular hair. Mucilage firm. Cushions 1mm to 2 or more cm wide .... **Chaetophora (see 16)**
    (b) Cushions generally smaller (up to about 5mm in diameter). Filaments with less branches, and cells rounded or with swollen ends. .... **Gongrosira**
    Gongrosira forms small green cushions on stones, plants etc. Cells 5–25µm broad 2–5 × lab. Filaments arise from a basal prostrate group of cells. The end cells can be swollen to form zoosporangia. Frequent in streams (particularly hard water) when mucilage can become calcified. (Plate II.8). Chlorophyceae.
21. (a) Plants small, cells less than 5µm diameter, walls thin, highly branched, first crosswall of each branch often a small distance from branch origin Pyrenoids absent. .... **Microthamnion**
    Microthamnion consists of attached delicate branched filaments. Epiphytic but may be detached. Cells < 5µm broad up to × 4 lab cylindrical. Chloroplast parietal, bright green, no pyrenoid. Branches opposite or alternate not tapering markedly towards the apex. Commonest species **M.kuetzingianum** which grows in clearer shallow waters, often in softer peaty areas. (Plate III.1). Chlorophyceae.
    (b) Plants larger, cells > 7µm in diameter, first cross walls of each branch at origin of branch, pyrenoids present **22**
22. (a) Filaments and branches tapering gradually to a fine point .... **Stigeoclonium (see 17)**
    (b) Filament terminating abruptly, not tapering gradually, with rounded blunt end cell **23**

23. (a)   Branches usually short, sometimes only a single cell in length and almost rhizoidal. .... **Rhizoclonium**
Rhizoclonium forms coarse wiry filaments with, although not always, short sometimes rhizoidal branches. Cell walls robust. Cell elongate, cylindrical 10–40μm broad 2–8 × lab. Chloroplast net like with many pyrenoids. Only British species is **R.hieroglyphium** which is common in hard shallow waters where it is found in dense mats. Often found with and can be confused with **Cladophora**. (Plate III.2). Chlorophyceae.

23. (b)   Branches longer and often repeated branching may occur .... **Cladophora**
Cladophora is typically well branched but in gently flowing waters branching may be intermittent and difficult to find. The branches are alternate or opposite, dichotomous or even trichotomous. Cell wall robust. Cells 50–150μm broad up to × 10 lab. Chloroplast net-like, parietal, with numerous pyrenoids (sometimes appearing to fill whole cell). Commonly known as blanket weed it can form extensive, coarse to touch green mats. Frequent in hard or semi-hard waters especially those enriched with sewage. When present in large amounts has been reported as imparting taste and odour to the water. Species of **Cladaphora** are not easy to separate but two forms seem to be common. **C.glomerata** is the commonest growing in large mats or strands many tens of centimetres long. Filaments well branched especially towards the apices – hard enriched waters. **C.sauteri** is less common forming tufted radiating cushions in hard water lakes – filaments less branched. (Plate III.3). Chlorophyceae.

24. (a)   Cells with siliceous wall **25**
   (b)   Cells without siliceous wall **29**
25. (a)   Cells embedded in a gelatinous tube but separate from each other within flat tube.
          Frustulia (in part see also 161)
          Cymbella (in part see also 148)
   (b)   Cells not as above **26**
26. (a)   Cells forming a continuous filament not surrounded by extensive mucilage. Cells normally seen in girdle view but if seen individually in valve view are completely circular (see glossary and introduction on description of diatom frustule). .... **Melosira**
Frustules of **Melosira** are cylindrical appearing circular in valve view and roughly rectangular in girdle view (the normal view under the microscope). Spines may or may

21

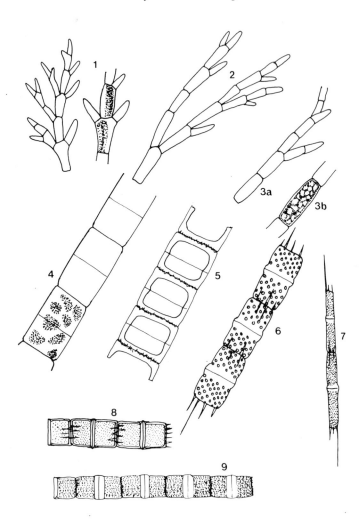

Plate III. 1. Microthamnion keutzingianum. 2. Rhizoclonium hieroglyphium. 3. Cladophora; (a) filament, (b) detail of cell. 4. Melosira varians. 5. Melosira arenaria. 6. Aulacoseira (Melosira) granulata. 7. Aulacoseira (Melosira) granulata var. angustissima. 8. Aulacoseira (Melosira) islandica. 9. Aulacoseira (Melosira) italica.

not be present around the end of the cell. If present they may be quite long or merely small teeth. Most species have some decoration on the valve face but this is not normally seen. When seen in girdle view most species show a furrow (sulcus) between the valve and the girdle bands. Five species commonly occur in freshwater and are separated on markings, spines and size. Bacillariophyceae.

NB. Cells of certain centric diatoms such as **Stephanodiscus** can be loosely held together with spines forming filament like chains. These more readily break up than true filaments of **Melosira** and when viewed on the valve surface often have more distinct patterns of dots present (see Plates XX and XXI for comparison). Some species of **Melosira** have been re-named **Aulacoseira** (Hartley 1986). They are all included in the same section of this key and changes of name are indicated.

i(a) Surface of frustule smooth .... **Melosira varians**
M.varians filaments often appear dark brown because of pigmentation in the plate like chloroplasts. Up to 40μm in diameter lab 1.5. Common in shallow still waters especially if eutrophic. (Plate III.4).

(b) Surface frustule with fine or coarse dots (may need acid cleaned frustules to see) .... **ii**

ii(a) Sulcus present .... **iii**

(b) Sulcus absent .... **Melosira arenaria**
M.arenaria has cylindrical cells up to 90μm broad with distinctly punctate walls, the puncta forming intersecting rows cross-hatching the surface. Ends of valves show fine teeth. Common in shallow water covering rocks, especially sandstone. (Plate III.5)

iii(a) Valves 5–20μm diameter, 1.5–2 lab, punctae fairly coarse, end cells usually have one or two longer robust spines in addition to shorter spines. .... **Aulacoseira granulata**
A.granulata is common in the plankton of lakes or in pools. Chloroplasts plate like greenish golden brown. (Plate III.6)
A.granulata v angustissmia is a common plankton variety, especially in eutrophic waters. It has much narrower cells (5–6μm diameter) which are 7–10 lab. The filaments are much finer. End cells have one or two finer long spines protruding. (Plate III.7).

(b) Valves without long spines protruding from end of filament .... **iv**

23

iv(a) Valves 7–27μm diameter 2–2.5 lab. Punctae finer than **A.granulata** forming rows (striae) parallel to long (pervalvar) axis. .... **Aulacoseira islandica** Found in lakes and rivers (Plate III.8). End spines fine and short. Sulcus obvious, broader.

(b) Valves 5–28μm diameter 2–2.7 lab. End spines short but distinct. Sulcus narrow puncta fine. ... **Aulacoseira italica** Common in plankton, chloroplasts plate like and green to golden brown. (Plate III.9).

26. (b) Cells forming a ribbon or chain but cells not circular in cross section **27**

27. (a) Cells with internal septa or costae **28**

(b) Cells without internal septa .... **Fragilaria** In **Fragilaria** the pennate or elongate frustules are joined by their valve faces to form a ribbon like chain. Valves fusiform sometimes slightly swollen at centre (gibbous) or with swollen (capitate) ends. Usually seen in girdle view in non-acid cleaned material. Valves striated – striae fine. The commoner species are indicated below. Bacillariophyceae.

i(a) Frustules joined along their entire valve face .... **ii**

(b) Frustules joined at valve centre only giving a comb like appearance to the ribbon. Frustule with slightly swollen centred and ends, 40–150μm broad. Striae 15–18 in 10μm. .... **F.crotonensis** Normally seen in girdle view but if cleaned may be seen in valve view when a clear rectangular area with no striae will be seen. Abundant in plankton of mesotrophic and eutrophic lakes. (Plate IV.1).

ii(a) Frustules markedly swollen when seen in valve view. Pseudoraphe broader at centre. Valves 7–25μm long 5–12μm broad. Striae fine 14–17 in 10μm and slightly acute near centre. .... **F. construens** A common species occurring both in the benthos and plankton (Plate IV.2).

(b) Frustule at most slightly swollen at centre when seen in valve view, otherwise linear .... **iii**

iii(a) Valves 3–25μm long 2–6μm wide, striae coarse 10–12 in 10μm, rectangular in girdle view. .... **F.pinnata** Widely distributed benthic (Plate IV.3).

(b) Valves longer, up to 120μm or more. Striae 12–19 in 10μm finer .... **iv**

iv(a) Central area rectangular clear of striae. Valves 25–100μm long 2–5μm wide. Striae delicate and parallel **F.capucina** Abundant benthic form can be seen in plankton (Plate IV.4).

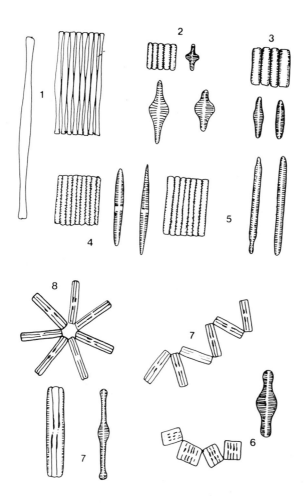

Plate IV. 1. Fragilaria crotonensis. **2.** F.construens. **3.** F.pinnata. **4.** F.capucina. **5.** F.virescens. **6.** Tabellaria flocculosa; (a) colony, (b) cell in valve view. **7.** Tabellaria fenestrata; (a) colony, (b) cell in valve view, (c) celling girdle view. **8.** Tabellaria fenestrata var. asterionelloides.

iv(b)   No clear central area. Valves 10–120μm long 3.7μm broad .... **F. virescens.** Common benthic form (Plate IV.5).

28. (a)   Cells rectangular or trabular in normal view, often united into zig-zag colonies. When seen individually valves show strongly swollen middle region. Cells with easily seen septa. .... **Tabellaria** In **Tabellaria** the frustules may form zig-zag or stellate colonies which are commonly seen in girdle view. Two common species occur. **T.flocculosa** has valves about 4–5 lab (12–50μm long, 5–16μm broad) with many internal septa (Plate IV.6) whereas **T.fenestrata** has much longer thinner cells (30–140μm long, 3–9μm broad) 6–10 lab and with fewer internal septa (Plate IV.7). Both are common in the plankton but **T.fenestrata** tends to prefer softer waters. **T.fenestrata** var. **asterionelloides** can be confused with **Asterionella** as it forms star shaped colonies (Plate IV.8) and can be common in larger nutrient poor waters. Bacillariophyceae.

(b)   Cells rectangular, may unite to form zig-zag colonies. Valves rod shaped and when seen individually show at the most a slightly swollen centre. Cells with transverse costae .... **Diatoma** **Diatoma** forms ribbon shaped or zig-zag colonies. Frustules have transverse internal costae which can be seen as ridges or points at the cell margin. Three species are common.

(i)(a)   Frustules long and slender 50–120μm long only 2–4μm wide. Internal costae narrow .... **Diatoma elongatum** **D.elongatum** (Plate V.1) is common in the plankton. Tends to form zig-zag colonies which can be confused with **Asterionella** but inner ends of cells not as swollen.

(b)   Frustules usually shorter (less than 100μm) and much broader (3–8 lab) .... **(ii)**

(ii)(a)   Frustules 25–100μm long, 7–20μm broad (4–8 lab). Costae robust (2–4 in 10μm). Frustules much broader at centre than end when seen in valve view .... **D. hiemale** **D.hiemale** (Plate V.2) forms short ribbons. A smaller variety, **v.mesoden** has shorter cells (less than 30μm) and is quite broad in valve view. Both are common in the plankton and aquatic plants in hard waters.

(b)   Frustules 30–60μm long, 10–13μm broad (3–5 lab). Internal costae narrow (6–8 in 10μm) .... **D.vulgare** Common in hard water plankton (Plate V.3) and also in river plankton, especially early in the year.

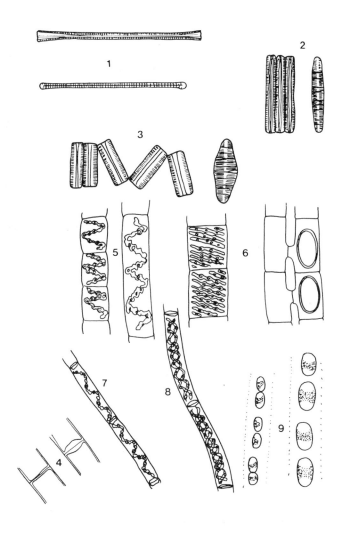

Plate V. 1. Diatoma elonagatum; (a) girdle view, (b) valve view. 2. Diatoma hiemale. 3. Diatoma vulgare. 4. Spirogyra (Condensata group). 5. S.condensata. 6. S.nitida. 7. S.inflata. 8. S.weberi. 9. Geminella.

29. (a)   Chloroplasts form a spiral band within the cell **Spirogyra**
Cells of **Spirogyra** are cylindrical with firm walls often
with a slimy outer coating of mucilage. Chloroplasts are
helical with up to 15 per cell. Numerous pyrenoids
present. Cell diameters range from 10–150μm depending
upon species and up to 200μm long. In shallow ponds and
ditches it can form dense green cushions or clouds. It is
found in a variety of waters, some species preferring hard
water and others rich in organic matter. Can impart a
grassy odour to the water. Chlorophyceae.
Identification of species can be difficult but four main
groups can be separated based on chloroplast number
and the structure of the cross-walls.

     (i)(a)   Cross walls simple – i.e. a single structure (see Plate
V.4) .... **(ii)**

        (b)   Cross walls replicate – i.e. where a collar of thickened
wall material occurs either side of the septum (see Plate
V.4) .... **(iii)**

     (ii)(a)   One chloroplast per cell . **Condensata group** (Plate V.5).

        (b)   2–16 chloroplasts per cell ...... **Crassa group** (Plate V.6).

     (iii)(a)   One chloroplast per cell .... **Inflata group** (Plate V.7).

        (b)   2–4 chloroplasts per cell, ... **Insignis group** (Plate V.8).

29. (b)   Chloroplasts not a spiral band **30**

30. (a)   Filaments embedded in a prominent broad hyaline
cylindrical mucilaginous envelope. Cells short cylinders
with broadly rounded ends often separate from one
another within the filaments. .... **Geminella**
Geminella cells are between 5–20μm broad (1–2 lab).
Chloroplast a parietal plate roughly saddle shaped and
near centre of cell, usually with pyrenoid. Occurs in
shallower waters, usually more acidic, often with **Sphagnum**. (Plate V.9). Chlorophyceae.

       (b)   Filaments not embedded in prominent mucilaginous
envelope **31**

31. (a)   Filament outline with constrictions giving toothed appearance **32**

       (b)   Filament outline without constrictions **33**

32. (a)   Cells elliptical when viewed from top, no central gap
between adjoining cells, well defined constriction, toothed
margin of filament with rounded "teeth" .. **Spondylosium**
Spondylosium is a filamentous desmid. Each cell of
filament has a fairly deep narrow constriction, one
chloroplast and pyrenoid in each semicell. Two common
species, **S.planum** is larger (cells 12–19μm broad) and
S.papilosum smaller (cells 8–9μm broad). Both occur

in upland areas around lake margins. (Plate VI.1). Chlorophyceae.

32. (b)   Cells angular (rarely elliptical) when viewed from top, small lens shaped gap between adjacent cells usually visible, constriction small, toothed margin with more angular "teeth". .... **Desmidium**
Desmidium is a filamentous desmid. Cells can form long twisted filaments enclosed in gelatinous envelope. Filaments may be triangular in cross section. One chloroplast and pyrenoid per semicell. Median constriction more notch-like. Two common species **D.aptogonum** (26–40μm broad) has spirally twisted filaments sometimes in a gelatinous sheath. **D.swartzii** also has spiral filaments (37–50μm broad) embedded in mucilage. Space between adjoining cells hardly noticeable. Common in vegetation and margins of oligotrophic lakes in mountainous areas. (Plate VI.2). Chlorophyceae.

33. (a)   Filaments very short, reduced to a few cells which easily disrupt into individual cells. Cells cylindrical with free ends rounded. .... **Stichococcus**
Stichococcus forms very reduced filaments, often of only 2–3 cells. Cells 2–6μm broad 32–12μm long. Single lobed chloroplast with no pyrenoid. On damp earth, tree trunks etc. sometimes washed into water courses. (Plate VI.3). Chlorophyceae.

(b)   Filaments not very short but typically many cells in length **34**

34. (a)   Large alga with tubular thallus many cells broad and long, macroscopic in size .... **Enteromorpha**
The body of **Enteromorpha** consists of a hollow tube of cells. The tube wall is one or two cells thick, many cells wide and long. The tubular thallus, which is characteristic, is deep green and is either attached or free floating. The tubes may branch and can be many centimetres in length. Although mainly salt water it occurs frequently in brackish and freshwaters particularly in rivers, ditches and lakes in southern England.
E.intestinalis is the commonest species. (Plate VI.4). Chlorophyceae.

(b)   Alga not a large tubular thallus: **35**

35. (a)   Chloroplasts two per cell and star shaped .... **Zygnema**
Cells of **Zygnema** are cylindrical and have two star shaped chloroplasts separated by a clear area each having a large central pyrenoid. Filaments usually with soft mucilaginous sheath. Cells 16–50μm diameter, 2–3 lab. Common

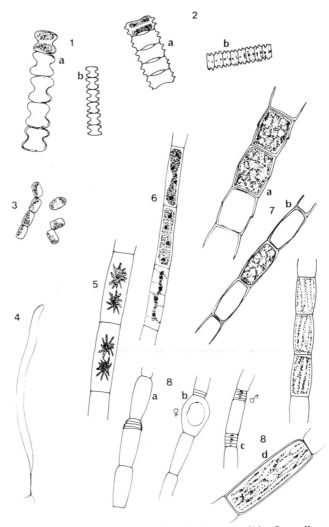

Plate VI. 1. Spondylosium; (a) S.planum, (b) S.papilosum.
2. Desmidium, (a) D.aptogonum, (b) D.swartzii. 3. Stichococcus.
4. Enteromorpha intestinalis. 5. Zygnema. 6. Mougeotia.
7. Micorspora; (a) M.amoena, (b) M.floccosa. 8. Oedogonium (a, b
& c) cap cell, male and female reproductive cells (d & e) vegetative
cells.

throughout Britain in shallow waters may form luxuriant growths. (Plate VI.5). Chlorophyceae.

35. (b)   Chloroplasts single or more than two per cell. **36**

36. (a)   Chloroplasts one per cell and in the form of a flat plate passing through the longitudinal axis of the cell ....

.... **Mougeotia**

Cells of **Mougeotia** have a flat plate-like chloroplast arranged along the long axis of the cells. When viewed face on, it appears to nearly fill the whole cell, but when viewed on edge it appears as a narrow central strand supported by cytoplasmic strands. The chloroplasts change their position in response to light so a number of cells may need to be viewed to see both face and edge views of the chloroplast. Species identification can only be made on fertile material which is not common. Cells 3.5–35μm diameter, 5–12 lab. Several pyrenoids per cell. Common in many habitats, especially upland regions. (Plate VI.6).

(b)   Chloroplast not as above **37**

37. (a)   Chloroplast reticulate (see glossary) **38**

(b)   Chloroplast not reticulate **40**

38. (a)   Cell walls thick, often lamellate, made of two overlapping halves which can break into H shaped pieces. End cells usually with H shaped ends. Pyrenoids absent. **Microspora**

Cell walls of **Microspora** are characteristically lamellate and formed of two overlapping halves shaped like H-pieces. Chloroplasts reticulate and not well defined although they may be thickened in some places to form parietal cushions. Cells 5–30μm diameter, 1–3 lab. Three common species, **M.amoena** (cells over 20μm diameter), **M.floccosa** (cells 7–15μm diameter) and with thinner walls and **M.spirogyroides**, a similar size but with a parietal chloroplast which is more banded. (Plate VI.7). Common but not abundant in smaller water bodies. More frequent at cooler times of the year. Chlorophyceae.

(b)   Cell wall not thick and lamellate and not composed of H-pieces. Pyrenoids present **39**

39. (a)   Cells cylindrical or swollen, cell walls robust. Cells 20–80μm broad, 5–15 lab. ..... **Cladophora** (in part see 23b).

(b)   Cells cylindrical, sometimes swollen slightly at one end, wall firm. Some cells have one or more ring-like transverse lines at swollen end of some cells. Cells 10–40μm broad 2–5 lab. .... **Oedogonium**

Cells of **Oedogonium** form long, unbranched filaments. Chloroplast parietal and net-like. Several pyrenoids present. Species identification only possible with fertile plants which are not always common. Over 200 species have been described, most are abundant in still or slow moving waters. When unattached they form dense pale-green masses. (Plate VI.8). Chlorophyceae.

40. (a)   Chloroplast ring or plate-shaped extending 1/3 to most way round the cell. One or more pyrenoids, starch test +ve **41**

    (b)   Cells cylindrical or slightly barrel shaped, 2–6 lab. Chloroplasts one to many rounded or platelet shaped. Cell walls may fragment into H-pieces. Starch −ve. ....

.... **Tribonema**

Cells of **Tribonema** form unbranched filaments of cylindrical or slightly barrel shaped cells. Walls are of 2–piece construction with H-pieces which are evident if cells break or at end of filaments. Chloroplasts disc or small plate-like shapes. Four species are common in lakes and reservoirs especially those richer in organic matter and humic materials. Xanthophyceae.

    (i)(a)   Cells narrow 5–7μm diameter 1–4 chloroplasts per cell . **(ii)**
    (b)   Cells broad, greater than 7μm diameter(7–20μm), slightly barrel shaped, chloroplasts numerous. .... **(iii)**

    (ii)(a)   Cells cylindrical not constricted at cross walls 5–5.6μm wide up to 8 lab. Chloroplasts 2–4 folded plate-like. ....
.... **T.affine**

T.affine is very common in small water bodies. (Plate VII.1). Cells 5–5.6μm wide 30–40μm long.

    (b)   Cells with slight constrictions at cross walls 3–6μm wide up to 6 lab .... **T.minus**

Cells of **T.minus** are 23–27μm long with 1–4 large disc or plate-like chloroplasts arranged parietally around the cell. Common in shallow lakes and ponds. (Plate VII.2).

    (iii)(a)   Cells 8–20μm wide, 2.5–8 lab numerous chloroplasts ......
.... **T.viride**

T.viride is comon in lakes and can form large growths which block filters at water treatment works. (Plate VII.3).

    (b)   Cells 6–11μm diameter, 2–3.5 lab. Chloroplasts 4–8 disc shaped. .... **T.bombycinum**

Although **T.bombycinum** chloroplasts are usually disc shaped in preserved material and in live, where the discs touch they appear to be 2–3 plates. Common in lakes and reservoirs. Can cause filtration problems. (Plate VII.4).

41. (a)   Chloroplast extending more than half way round cell usually nearly completely covering inside of wall. ....
.... **Ulothrix**

Cells of **Ulothrix** are cylindrical either longer or shorter than broad depending upon species one to several pyrenoids. **U.zonata** has cells 11–37μm wide, usually shorter than broad with thick walls. There are up to 8 pyrenoids for each chloroplast. Filaments attached by small holdfast or free floating. **U.aequalis** forms very long filaments of cells 13–15μm broad and 18–30μm long. Commonly forms bright green floating masses in shallow waters. (Plate VII.5 & 6). Chlorophyceae.

41. (b)   Chloroplast extending less than half way round cell. .... **Hormidium** Cylindrical cells 5–15μm broad, 1–3 lab. Parietal band or plate-like chloroplast extending less than half way round cell with (usually) single pyrenoid. Common on damp soil and acidic streams. Filaments may easily fragment. (Plate VII.7). Chlorophyceae.

42. (a)   Plant filamentous but without true branching. Sometimes false branching may be present (see glossary) **43**

    (b)   Filaments with true branching .... **Stigonema** **Stigonema** grows as filaments up to 70μm wide, the main axis of which may be multiseriate and the side branches of which are uniseriate. Occasional heterocysts. A firm mucilaginous sheath is present which is often stained yellowish brown in colour. Grows as a thin mat over stones, rocks, damp soil or damp trees but can break away to be free floating. (Plate VII.10).

43. (a)   False branching present **44**

    (b)   False branching absent (or only occasional in **Rivularia** which is distinguished by its tapering trichomes) **45**

44. (a)   Branches arise in pairs, often a few cells away from a heterocyst .... **Scytonema** Filaments of **Scytonema** (Plate VII.8) are sheathed, the sheath often being quite thick. False branches develop in pairs between heterocysts (rarely singly and rarely next to heterocysts). Trichomes uniseriate (solitary) within sheath. Homogonia form in the branches. Cells in shape of short cylinders, 8–15μm diameter. Filaments (i.e. including sheath) up to 60μm in diameter. Common species include **S.mirarbile** and **S.alatum**. Found growing on rocks, submerged macrophytes etc., as felt-like masses. Species in hard water areas may have sheaths encrusted with lime. Cyanobacteria.

    (b)   Branches single (usually) arising just below a heterocyst . ... **Tolypothrix**

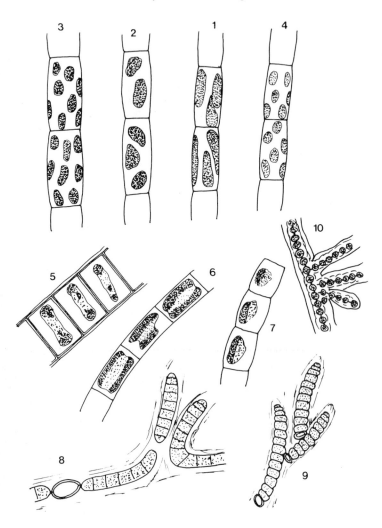

Plate VII. 1. Tribonema affine. 2. T.minus. 3. T.viride. 4. T.bombycinum. 5. Ulothrix zonata. 6. U.æqualis. 7. Hormidium. 8. Scytonema. 9. Tolypothrix. 10. Stigonema.

Tolypothrix filaments have sheaths of varying thickness, uniseriate. Can be solitary or forming tufts in which filaments more or less radiate from a central point. False branches arise from just below a heterocyst. Cells short cylinders, square or barrel shaped sometimes with constrictions at cross-walls. Sheath firm if thin but may be gelatinous or lamellate if thicker. Gonidia oval or elliptical often occurring in a series. Cells 5–13μm wide, filaments up to 17μm wide. Common species include **T.lanata** which grows on rocks and plants in softer water areas and **T.tenuis** which forms attached or free floating tufts in both hard and soft waters. (Plate VII.9). Cyanobacteria.

45. (a)   Heterocysts present (although sometimes infrequent)   **46**

(b)   Heterocysts always absent **51**

46. (a)   Trichome gradually tapering to a point at one end. Globular or spherical colonies, attached or free floating. **47**

(b)   Trichomes approximately the same width throughout   **48**

47. (a)   Trichomes with basal heterocyst adjacent to which are cylindrical gonidia. Mucilage soft, globular. Trichomes radially arranged. Usually free floating ...... **Gloeotrichia** **Gloeotrichia** (Plate VIII.1) forms globular, usually free floating masses. Trichomes radiate from centre and sheath often only obvious near base of trichome. Trichomes strongly tapering. Heterocysts solitary, globular. Gonidia cylindrical usually adjoining heterocyst. **G.pisum** forms brownish to olive green colonies in harder waters which may be attached when young and do not usually reach more than 2mm in diameter. **G.natans** forms larger (up to 10cm) colonies which are soft and gelatinous and, again, brownish to olive green. Attached when young, free floating later – in harder waters. Softness of colonies means they easily break up in rough waters forming more irregular shapes. **G.pisum** is associated with the breaking of the meres the formation of dense blooms in the Shropshire and Cheshire meres. Cyanobacteria.

(b)   Trichomes with basal heterocyst but without gonidia attached – mucilage firm .... **Rivularia** Trichomes of **Rivularia** have a radial or parallel arrangement within copious but firm mucilage. Forms attached, globose colonies which may get hollow when older. Some false branching may occur. Heterocysts basal. Common species include **R.haematites** and **R.minutula**. (Plate VIII.2). Cyanobacteria.

48. (a)   Heterocysts terminal, gonidia ellipsoidal to ovate adjoining heterocyst .... **Cylindrospermum** **Cylindrospermum** is characterised by its terminal heterocysts which may be at one or both ends of the trichomes. Trichomes usually loosely tangled in soft mucilage and growing on damp soil, stones etc. Cells 3.5–6μm diameter, 4–13μm long. **C.majus** is found in soft waters and is slightly smaller than another common species **C.stagnale**. (Plate VIII.3). Cyanobacteria.

(b)   Heterocysts not terminal but intercalary **49**

49. (a)   End cells of filament elongated and slightly narrowing when compared with the rest of the trichome. Gonidia, when present, solitary. .... **Aphanizomenon** Trichomes of **Aphanizomenon** are grouped together in parallel to form bundles or rafts often visible to the naked eye. Planktonic. Trichomes relatively short tapering slightly at both ends. Cells rectangular, 5–6μm diameter, 8–12μm long with slight constrictions at cross walls. Heterocysts cylindrical, 7μm diameter, 12–20μm long, located in the middle of a trichome. Gonidia also cylindrical and in the mid region but not adjacent to heterocysts, 8μm diameter, 60–70μm long. One species only, **A.flos-aquae**, which is common in the plankton especially those rich in nutrients where it can form dense blooms. More common in harder waters. (Plate VIII.4). Cyanobacteria.

(b)   End cells of trichomes not narrower than the rest **50**

50. (a)   Trichomes solitary or in a tangled formless mass. .... **Anabaena** Trichomes of **Anabaena** are uniformly broad throughout and embedded in amorphous and sometimes inconspicuous soft mucilage. Filaments straight or coiled. Cells rounded or barrel shaped (rarely cylindrical). Heterocysts spherical. Gonidia rounded or cylindrical. Cyanobacteria. Common species may be separated as follows:

(i)(a)   Planktonic .... **(ii)**

(b)   Not planktonic but forming layer over surface of soil, plants or other substrate .... **(iv)**

(ii)(a)   Trichomes coiled or spiral .... **(iii)**

(b)   Trichomes irregularly twisted. Gonidia sausage shaped and formed near centre of tangled filaments often adjacent to heterocysts. .... **A.flos-aquae** **A.flos-aquae** is abundant in lakes, especially hard water ones, where it may form blooms and surface scums frequently in association with **Microcystis**. Cells spherical,

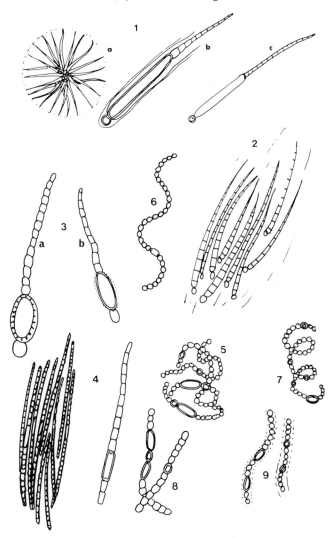

Plate VIII. 1. Gloeotrichia pisum; (a) colony, (b) filament, (c) G.natans. 2. Rivularia. 3. Cylindrospermum; (a) C.stagnale, (b) C.majus. 4. Aphan izomenon flos-aquae; (a) raft, (b) trichome. 5. Anabaena flos-aquae. 6. A.spiroides. 7. A.circinalis. 8. A.oscillarioides. 9. A.inaequalis.

often with granular contents and conspicuous pseudovacuoles, 4–8μm broad. Heterocysts globular 79μm broad, 6–10μm long. Has been assciated with fish mortalities. (Plate VIII.5).

(iii)(a)   Trichomes forming a definite coil or spiral ...   **A.spiroides**
Cells of **A.spiroides** are roughly spherical, 6.5–8μm diameter. Heterocysts spherical about 7μm in diameter. Gonidia 14μm diameter and spherical often adjacent to heterocysts. Abundant in plankton can form blooms. Typical spiral trichomes with thin mucilaginous sheath. (Plate VIII.6).

(b)   Trichomes more irregularly coiled not a distinct spiral ....
.... **A.circinalis**
A.circinalis has spherical cells 8–14μm diameter. Heterocysts also spherical 8–10μm diameter. Gonidia remote from heterocysts, cylindrical 1418μm wide and 22–32μm long. Very common, often grows in association with **A.spiroides** and **Microcystis**. Forms water blooms in richer harder water lakes. (Plate VIII.7).

(iv)(a)   Cells roughly barrel shaped 4–6μm diameter gonidia cylindrical either side of heterocysts. ..... **A.oscillarioides**
Found in still waters forming films over vegetation, rocks and soil. Trichomes straight, solitary or twisted in thin gelatinous layer. Heterocysts rounded or ovate 6–8μm diameter. Gonidia cylindrical 8–14μm wide 20–60μm long. (Plate VIII.8).

(b)   Cells barrel shaped 35–5μm diameter. Gonidia cylindrical scattered along filament .... **A.inaequalis**
Found amongst other algae or on other substratum. Trichomes straight or twisted enclosed by sticky sheath. Heterocysts globose 4–6μm diameter, 7μm long. Gonidia scattered along filament 6–8μm diameter 15–16μm long – sometimes golden brown in colour. (Plate VIII.9).

50. (b)   Trichomes embedded in firm mucilage of definite shape which does not change when disturbed. .... **Nostoc**
Cells of **Nostoc** are similar to **Anabaena** but the trichomes are embedded in a firm mucilaginous surround. Five common species. Cyanobacteria.

(i)(a)   Forming bright blue spherical colonies 5–10μm diameter – planktonic .... **N.coeruleum**
Occurs in quiet eutrophic waters. Trichomes densely tangled. Cells roughly spherical or slightly barrel shaped 5–7μm diameter. Heterocysts frequent 8–10μm diameter. (Plate IX.1).

(b)   Not as above .... **(ii)**

(ii)(a) Forming large soft unstructured mass trichomes not densely coiled .... **N.piscinale**
Widely distributed in ponds and ditches or in damp rocks or soil. Cells 3–7μm broad, 1–2 lab. Heterocysts roughly spherical to oblong 4.5–6μm broad. Spores with hyaline wall, in chains, 6–7μm wide. (Plate IX.2).

(b) Forming firmer more structured mass. Trichomes densely tangled or radiating in spherical colony. .... **(iii)**

(iii)(a) Trichomes in tough, thick, warty mucilage, solid when young, hollow when older. Olive green to brown in colour. Attached or free .... **N.verrucosum**
N.verrucosum is commonly found on the beds of faster flowing rivers but also in medium hardness lakes. Cells compressed to spherical 3–4μm diameter. Heterocysts a similar shape but larger (6μm diameter). Gonidia ovate 5 × 7μm. (Plate IX.3).

(b) Not enveloped in thick warty mucilage .... **(iv)**

(iv)(a) Normally planktonic forming spherical colonies ....
.... **N.pruniforme**
Trichomes entangled in copious but firm mucilage. Olive green to black in colour. Free living spherical colonies but may be attached when young. Free colonies up to one cm diameter. Cells spherical or barrel shaped 4–6μm diameter, 4–7μm long. Heterocysts globose 6–7μm diameter. Gonidia spherical, 10μm diameter. Common in hard waters. Round colonies can be abundant on bottoms of ponds or small lakes where they roll around. (Plate IX.4).

(b) Not planktonic but forming flat membranous encrusting colony .... **N.commune**
Flat leathery membranous colonies can be many centimetres in diameter – blue green, olive green or brown. Trichomes tangled. Cells 4–6μm wide nearly spherical. Heterocysts 7μm wide. Found on moist soils or wet surfaces. (Plate IX.5).

51. (a) Trichomes form a regular spirally coiled cylinder in which individual cells are not obvious. .... **Spirulina**
Trichomes twisted to form a regular spiral. Cross walls obscure, difficult to see. Often have frequent gas vacuoles. Frequent, though not abundant in Britain. **S.subsalsa** has trichomes 1–2μm broad irregularly coiled in stagnant and 0sometimes brackish waters. **S.major** trichomes are 1–2μm broad but regularly coiled and found in stagnant fresh waters. **S.platensis** has trichomes 6–8μm wide and regularly coiled. It is common, sometimes forming blooms

in alkaline slightly salty tropical and sub-tropical lakes. (Plate IX.6). **Arthrospira** and **Spirulina** are similar shapes but the former is separated by some authors as having obvious cross-walls. Cyanobacteria.

51. (b)   Trichomes not forming a regular definite spiral, individual cells of trichome usually more easy to distinguish with care **52**

52. (a)   Trichomes without a sheath .... **Oscillatoria** Trichomes can be free floating and planktonic or woven as a thin covering to a substratum. Edges of trichome usually form unbroken parallel lines although some species do show constrictions at cross walls. Trichomes often very long. Gliding movement are common. Gas vacuoles common in planktonic forms. Shape of end cell of filament can be an important identification feature as well as size. Some of the more common species are indicated below. Cyanobacteria.

   (i)(a)   Trichomes more than 25μm diameter .... **O.princeps** Large broad trichomes 25–50μm diameter not constricted at cross walls. Solitary or loosely tangled small floating masses. Dark green-black in colour. Trichomes are slightly tapering towards the apex with slightly capitate end cell. Fresh or brackish water, common but not abundant. (Plate IX.7).

    (b)   Trichomes less than 20μm diameter .... **(ii)**

  (ii)(a)   Trichomes 11–20μm diameter .... **O.limosa** Trichomes composed of cells 11–20μm diameter with no constrictions, or at most very slight constrictions, at cross walls. Cells 1/6 – 1/3 lab, cross walls granulated. End cell flatly rounded. Trichome dark blue-green to brown. Very common in stagnant or standing waters, fresh or brackish. (Plate IX.8).

    (b)   Trichomes less than 10μm diameter .... **(iii)**

 (iii)(a)   Trichomes less than 2μm diameter .... **(iv)**

    (b)   Trichomes between 4–10μm diameter .... **(v)**

  (iv)(a)   Trichomes 1.5 – 1.8μm diameter, 2–6 lab, apical cell bluntly rounded. Slight constriction at cross walls .... **O.limnetica** Solitary straight or slightly curved trichomes with noticeable but slight constrictions at cross walls. No capitate end cell, no calyptra. Cross walls not granular. Planktonic often mixed with other algae. Pale blue-green. (Plate IX.9).

    (b)   Trichomes 0.8 – 2μm wide 2–5 lab. Apical cell bluntly rounded but constrictions at cross walls more marked .....

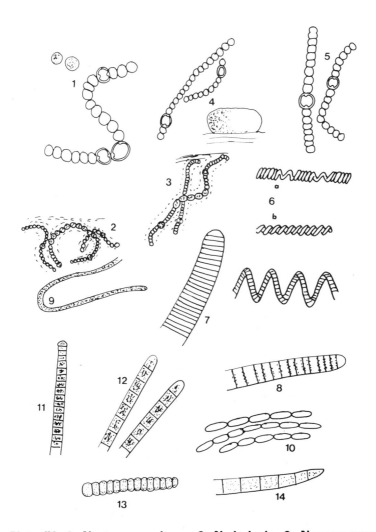

Plate IX. 1. Nostoc coeruleum. 2. N.piscinale. 3. N.verrucosum.
4. N.pruniforme. 5. N.commune. 6. Spirulina; (a) S.subsalsa,
(b) S.major, (c) S.platensis. 7. Oscillatoria princeps. 8. O.limosa.
9. O.limnetica. 10. O.redekii. 11. O.rubescens. 12. O.agardhii.
13. O.tenuis. 14. O.brevis.

.... **O.redekii**
A common planktonic form with marked constriction at
cross walls. Cells with gas vacuoles. End cell rounded no
calyptra. (Plate IX.10).

(v)(a)   Apical cell capitate often with calyptra. Trichomes 6–8μm
broad slightly tapering. .... **O.rubescens**
O.rubescens has distinctly red to purple trichomes which
very slightly taper at the end where the end cell is
capitate. Cells 6–8μm broad 1/3 – 1/2 lab with gas
vacuoles. Not constricted at cross walls. Very common
planktonic species in eutrophic waters forming purplish
red floating masses, even in the winter and under ice.
(Plate IX.11).

(b)   Apical cells not capitate, no calyptra .... **(vi)**

(vi)(a)   Cone shaped apical cell at end of briefly tapering
trichome. Cells 4–6μm, 3/4 lab, gas vacuoles present ......
.... **O.agardhii**
Trichomes not constricted at cross walls which are
granular. Cells only just wider than long. Trichomes form
blue-green masses either attached or free floating –
common. (Plate IX.12).

(b)   Apical cell not cone shaped, cells much broader than
long (1/3–1/2 lab) .... **(vii)**

(vii)(a)   Cells 4–10μm diameter, cross walls not or only slightly
constricted, granular; apical cell rounded. Trichomes not
attenuated at ends. .... **O.tenuis**
Common on damp surfaces or in plankton especially in
ponds and shallow pools where it forms bluegreen or
olive-green masses. (Plate IX.13).

(b)   Cells 4–6μm diameter. Trichomes briefly attenuated
towards end. End wall rounded. Not constricted at cross
walls, no granulation. .... **O.brevis**
O.brevis forms olive-green to blue-green coverings to
damp surfaces. No gas vacuoles. .... (Plate IX.14)

52. (b)   Trichomes surrounded by a sheath **53**
53. (a)   Trichomes single or free. Sheath delicate but firm (very
occasionally thick) .... **Lyngbya**
Filaments of **Lyngbya** are formed of uniseriate cells
enclosed by a more or less firm sheath. They can be
solitary or aggregated together forming tangled masses
but sheaths do not become confluent. Free floating or
growing on a substrate. Sheaths may become yellowish-
brown. Two of the commoner species are **L.versicolor**
which has small cells 2.8–3.4μm diameter and a sheath up
to 2μm thick. Trichomes not constricted at the cross walls

and cross walls not granular. **L.versicolor** grows on submerged structures but may detach and float free. (Plate X.1). **L.aerugineo-caerulea** has larger cells, 4–7μm diameter but with a relatively firm sheath. Found attached or free floating in a variety of lakes. (Plate X.2). Cyanobacteria.

53. (b) Filaments interwoven in a sticky gelatinous matrix, sheaths of trichomes sticky and sometimes indistinct ....
.... **Phormidium**

Phormidum is extremely common on damp soil, rocks, streams, ponds etc. Trichomes cylindrical and may taper slightly towards the end. Cells shorter than wide. Because of the difficulty in seeing the sheath when preserved it can be confused with **Oscillatoria**. Two of the more common species are **P.autumnale** which has a capitate apical cell with calyptra, cells 4–7μm broad and it is common on damp soil and **P.tenue** which has a conical apical cell without a calyptra, cells 1–3μm broad and forms blue-green masses amongst the algae and submerged aquatics. (Plate X.3 & 4). Cyanobacteria.

54. (a) Cell pigments not localized in chloroplasts. **55**
    (b) Cell pigments localized in chloroplasts ...:................ **64**
55. (a) Epiphytic, unicellular or at most a few celled colony which has exospores produced at apical end. ....
.... **Chamaesiphon**

Chamaesiphon is epiphytic on other aquatic plants after forming dense aggregates. Cells usually sausage shaped, sometimes bent, 10–50μm long, 2–7μm wide. Cells usually surrounded by a sheath which may be brownish in colour. Exospores are produced at apex of mother cell, 2–5μm diameter spherical, produced in single or multiple rows. **C.incrustans** has single rows, **C.confervicola** has multiple rows. (Plate X.5 & 6). Common. Cyanobacteria.

    (b) Cells form colonies which are not epiphytic (can rarely have individual cells in Chroococcus but these are planktonic) **56**
56. (a) Cells arranged in a rectilinear series (see glossary), often in groups of four or many groups of four, in a plate one cell thick .... **Merismopedia**
Cells of **Merismopedia** spherical to oval in a single layer within structureless mucilage. Free floating or resting on the bottom sediments. Three of the more common species are as below:
Cyanobacteria.

(i)(a) Cells 3–4μm wide separated from each other by mucilage
.... **M.punctata**
(Plate X.7).

(b) Cells closely packed within mucilage .... **(ii)**

(ii)(a) Cells 5–7μm broad 5–9μm long, bright blue-green, often with coarse granulations .... **M.elegans**
M.elegans is the largest British species and may have many thousands of cells in a colony (Plate X.8). Common in still waters e.g. canals.

(b) Cells 3–6μm broad pale blue-green. .... **M.glauca**
Cells and colonies smaller than in **M.elegans**. (< cells/colony). Common. (Plate X.9).

56. (b) Cells not as above but in spherical, ovate or irregular colonies or as unicells **57**

57. (a) Cells in distinct colonies which form hollow spheres with cells arranged uniformly around the periphery **58**

(b) Cells individual or in colonies which are not hollow (at most clathrate – see glossary) and cells distributed throughout **59**

58. (a) Cells pear-shaped to sub-spherical, sometimes with mucilaginous sheaths and arranged at ends of branching strands of mucilage radiating from the colony centre ......
.... **Gomphosphaeria**
Gomphosphaeria is common in lakes and ponds and may be the dominant species. Two common species are **G.lacustris** which has cells 1.5–2.5μm broad and 2–4μm long. The cells have distinct gelatinised envelopes and are often arranged in clusters within the colony. Generally distributed but possibly with a preference for hard waters, and **G.aponina** which has larger pyriform cells, 4–12μm broad and 8–16μm long with a distinct envelope. Colonies large 40–90μm diameter (**G.lacustris** only 30μm diameter). Found commonly in ponds and ditches. (Plate X.10 & 11). Cyanobacteria.

58. (b) Cells spherical to oval, not at ends of radiating mucilaginous strands but merely embedded in an homogenous mucilaginous mass ....:... **Coelosphaerium**
Cells of **Coelosphaerium** are spherical to subspherical or even oval. Colonies are common in the plankton and may reach bloom proportions. Two species are common. **C.keutzingianum** has cells 2–5μm broad which are roughly spherical and rarely have gas vacuoles. Colonies 20–90μm broad. Widely distributed especially in the plankton of harder waters. **C.naegelianum** has ovoid to ellipsoidal cells 3–5μm broad and 5–7μm long. Gas vacuoles are

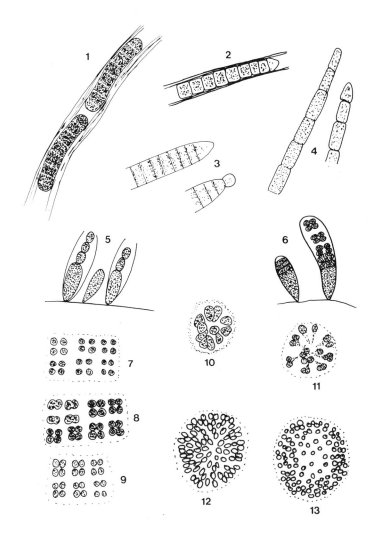

Plate X. 1. Lynbya versicolor. 2. L.coerulea. 3. Phormidium autumnale. 4. P.tenue. 5. Chamaesiphon incrustans. 6. C.convervicolor. 7. Merismopedia punctata. 8. M.elegans. 9. M.glauca. 10.Gomphosphaeria aponica. 11.G.lacustris. 12. Coelosphaerium keutzingianum. 13. C.naegelianum

common. Colonies 50–180µm diameter. Common bloom forming algae especially in richer harder waters. (Plate X.12 & 13). Cyanobacteria.

The distinction between **Gomphosphaeria** and (**Coelosphaerium** is not always clear but is based on cell shape and internal structure of colonies.

59. (a)   Cells forming small colonies of 2–4–8 or rarely 16–32 cells embedded in mucilage **60**

   (b)   Mucilaginous colonies composed of many cells – often hundreds **62**

60. (a)   Cells spherical or nearly so **61**

   (b)   Cells longer than broad – elongate .... **Synechococcus**
Cells of **Synechococcus** are ovoid to cylindrical 4–15µm broad and 2–10 lab. Cells either solitary or in twos or rarely fours. Mucilage envelope either thin or absent. Frequent in plankton and damp surfaces. **S.aeruginosa** is the commonest British species. (Plate X1.1). Cyanobacteria.

61. (a)   Cells with distinct envelope which is lamellate and usually thick .... **Gloeocapsa**
Gloeocapsa cells between one and 30µm in diameter and have sheaths up to 10µm thick. The sheaths vary in colour with species as does cell size. Globally abundant, especially on wet rocks. **G.turgida** has large cells (8–30µm) with colourless envelopes, **G.rupestris** has smaller cells 6–10µm diameter with a yellow-brown sheath and **G.alpina** has violet-blue sheaths and is 2–8µm diameter (Plate X1.2 to 3). Cyanobacteria.

   (b)   Cells nearly spherical, after division daughter cells in groups of 2–4 – 8–16 in gelatinous sheath often homogenous with surrounding mucilage but lamellate in some species .... **Chroococcus**
Chroococcus usually forms small groups of cells which are either free floating or attached. Planktonic species do not tend to have distinct sheaths but are confluent with the surrounding mucilage. Easily confused with **Gloeocapsa**. Two common species are **C.turgidus** which has large cells up to 32µm diameter and 2–4 cells in each sheath, bright blue green in colour and is common in lakes and in Sphagnum and **C.limneticus** which has smaller cells (up to 12µm) and is in groups of up to 32 with no distinct sheaths. Cells blue green in colour and common in plankton. (Plate XI.4 & 5). Cyanobacteria.

62. (a)   Large mucilaginous colonies, cells spherical. **63**

   (b)   Large mucilaginous colonies, cells cylindrical to elongate .... **Aphanothece**

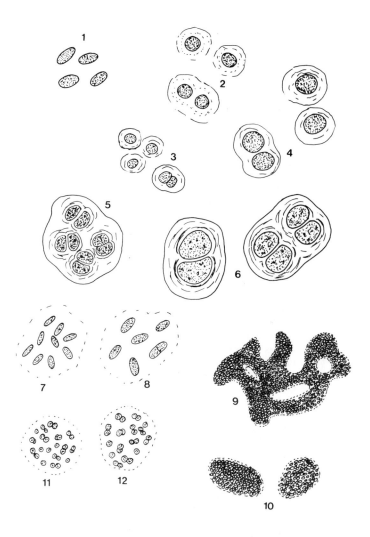

Plate XI. 1. **Gloecapsa turgida.** 2. **G.rupestris.** 3. **G.alpina.**
4. **Chroococcus turgidus.** 5. **C.limneticus.** 6. **Synechococcus aeruginosa.** 7. **Aphanothece saxicola.** 8. **A.microscopica.**
9. **Microcystis aeruginosa.** 10. **M.flos-aquae.** 11. **Aphanocapsa delicatissima.** 12. **A.grevallei.**

Cells of **Aphanothece** are ovate to cylindrical embedded in copious mucilage. Free floating or sedentary. **A.microscopica** (cells 3–4μm by 5–8 long) and **A.saxicola** (cells 1–2μ br and 2–6μm long) are common forms. The cells of both are pale blue-green and the colonies, especially of the latter, are easily mistaken for bacteria. Both are common in the plankton or margins of lakes and ponds. (Plate XI. 7.8). Cyanobacteria.

63. (a)   Cells of colony densely crowded within mucilagex .... **Microcystis** Cells of **Microcystis** are spherical to subspherical usually with gas vacuoles. They form larger globular to irregular colonies and are often responsible for water blooms some of which can result in animal mortalities. They can also impart taste and odour to the water. Two species common. **M.aerugineoa** has lobed, clathrate colonies with cells 3–5μm diameter and **M.flos-aquae** has globose colonies. Both are common in enriched and hard waters (Plate XI.9 & 10). Cyanobacteria.

(b)   Cells more spaced out within mucilage. ..... **Aphanocapsa** **Aphanocapsa** forms a globular amorphous gelatinous colony which is usually free floating. Cells much more spaced out than in **Microcystis** and also sometimes in pairs as a result of cell division. Two common species are **A.delicatissima** which has very small cells (<1μm diameter) and is common in the plankton and **A.grevellei** which has larger cells (3.5–5.5μm diameter) which may be planktonic or occur on damp soils. (Plate XI. 11 & 12). Cyanobacteria.

64. (a)   Cells arranged in colonies of definite shape **65**

(b)   Cells either individual, in pairs or in aggregations with no definite shape **102**

65. (a)   Cells of colony with flagella, colony motile **66**

(b)   Cells of colony without flagella, colony nonmotile **72**

66. (a)   Each cell in a vase shaped lorica with wide opening at one end .... **Dinobryon** (in part see 9)

(b)   Each cell not located in a lorica **67**

67. (a)   Adjacent cells touching in densely packed colonies ... **68**

(b)   Cells spaced apart within a colourless mucilaginous matrix **69**

68. (a)   Chloroplast green cup shaped, storage product starch, cells embedded in mucilage which obviously extends beyond colony, two equal length flagella .... **Pandorina** Colonies of **Pandorina** are spherical with 8–32 densely packed cells. The cells have flattened sides where they touch one another and slightly flattened apices. Cells

48

8–20 μm long. Outside the cells is a broad zone of clear mucilage through which the flagella protrude. There is no hollow at the centre of the colony. Individual cells may divide to form daughter colonies. Common throughout Britain. Colonies move with tumbling motion through the water. Commonest species **P.morum** (Plate XII.1). Chlorophyceae.

68. (b)   Chloroplasts brown to golden-brown. Storage product leucosin, no obvious broad mucilaginous envelope, two flagella of unequal length .... **Synura**
Cells of **Synura** have 10 golden-brown chloroplasts and are pear shaped 7–17 μm broad. Up to 40 cells per colony closely packed. The cells are covered with fine silica scales which are not always obvious. **S.ulvella** is common and may be seen swimming rapidly in the plankton of small lakes. It is noted for imparting a strong taste and odour to the water (Plate XII.2). Chrysophyceae.

69. (a)   Colonies of 64 cells or less **70**

    (b)   Colonies of considerably more than 64 cells – often over 100. .... **71**

70. (a)   Colony a flat plate of 4–16 (32) ovoid to spherical cells. Flagellae of colony all point to one side .... **Gonium**
Cells of **Gonium** are arranged in a flat rectangular gelatinous envelope, each having two equal flagella. Chloroplast green parietal cup with 1 or 2 pyrenoids. Storage product starch. Cells 7–20μm broad. Common in still waters. **G.pectorale** is the commonest species with usually 16 celled colonies and more spherical cells 7–12μm broad. **G.sociale** has 4 sub-spherical cells per colony 10–20μm in diameter. (Plate XII.3). Chlorophyceae.

    (b)   Colony globose to elliptical of 16–32 (64) cells. Cells spherical arranged near surface of mucilaginous matrix. Two equal flagella per cell which point in all directions from colony surface .... **Eudorina**
Unlike cells of **Pandorium**, those of **Eudorina** are spherical and spaced out in a mucilaginous matrix near the edge leaving a gap at the centre (they may be more closely packed in immature colonies. Chloroplasts cup shaped, one or more pyrenoids, storage product starch. **E.elegans** is the commonest species which has cells 16–25μm diameter. Widely distributed and can form dense growths in the summer. (Plate XII.4). Chlorophyceae.

71. (a)   Chloroplasts golden-brown. Cells pear shaped with thread-like mucilage strands connecting them to colony centre,

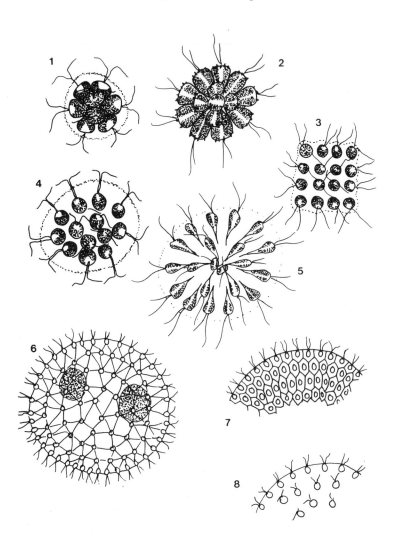

Plate XII. 1. Pandorina morum. 2. Synura ulvella. 3. Eudorina elegans. 4. Gonium pectorale. 5. Uroglena. 6. Volvox tertius. 7. V.aureus. 8. V.globator.

storage product leucosin. .... **Uroglena**
Colonies of **Uroglena** are large, up to 1mm diameter, and
containing many hundreds of cells. Cells 10–22μm long
with one or two chloroplasts. Cysts are produced which
have smooth walls and may or may not have a collar.
Each cell with two, unequal length, flagella. Although
similar, Uroglena colonies can be easily distinguished
from **Volvox** by the golden-brown chloroplasts, pear shaped
cells and unequal flagella. (Plate XII.5). Chrysophyceae.

71. (b) Chloroplasts green, storage product starch. Cells spherical,
with interconnecting protoplasmic strands or mucilaginous
network but these do not radiate from colony centre .....
.... **Volvox**
Volvox colonies are large and spherical with hundreds or
thousands of cells. Daughter colonies develop from special
cells within the hollow colony. Colonies can be up to
2.5mm in diameter. The three species common in Britain
can be separated thus:-

    i(a) Cells without interconnecting strands but separated by
polygonal mucilaginous network .... **V.tertius**
V.tertius has cells 4–8μm wide and between 500–2,000
per colony. Common (Plate XII.6).

    (b) Cells interconnected with mucilaginous strands .... **(ii)**
    ii(a) Cells 4–6μm diameter, colony 200–500μm diameter. Cells
usually rounded .... **V.aureus**
V.aureus has spherical colonies of, usually, more than
1000 cells. Common in lakes and ponds. (Plate XII.7).

    (b) Cells 2.5–5.5μm diameter, colony 600–800μm diameter,
1,500–25,000 cells which are of irregular shape ....
.... **V.globator**
Cells of **V.globator** have interconnections and surrounding
sheaths. Common in lakes and ponds early in the summer,
especially when nitrogen content is high. (Plate XII.8).

72. (a) Cells with silica walls which often bear distinct markings.
Storage products mainly oil not starch **73**

    (b) Cells without silica walls, main storage product starch **77**

73. (a) Cells (frustules) cuneate forming a fan shaped colony .....
.... **Meridion**
The frustules of **Meridion** are heteropolar in girdle view
and isobilateral in valve view. Within the frustule are
thickened transapical costae and on the surface fine
parallel striae. Pseudoraphe present on both valves.
Individuals usually unite to form a fan shaped, or if
growth is vigorous, a flat spiral shaped colony. Chloroplasts
numerous and plate-like. Frustules 24–45μm long. Often

abundant in still waters (e.g. ditches) or slow flowing waters especially early in the year. **Meridion circulare** is the only British species. (Plate XIII.1). Bacillariophyceae.

73. (b)   Cells (frustules) forming a stellate or zig-zag colonies **74**

74. (a)   Frustule swollen at each end to form a rounded knob. Colonies stellate .... **Asterionella** Frustules of **Asterionella** are long, straight and narrow with rounded ends. Heteropolar (with largest end to the "hub" of the colony) or nearly isopolar. Very narrow axial area and very fine, difficult to see, transverse striae. Usually two or more chloroplasts per cell. Frustules 40–130μm long up to 20 lab. **A.formosa** is abundant in the plankton of lakes, especially mesotrophic and eutrophic ones. Populations can frequently reach bloom proportions in the spring and autumn. During population growth silica is absorbed from the water and can become limiting causing numbers to decline. **Asterionella** is frequently associated with filter clogging and has been occasionally reported as causing taste and odours in water. (Plate XIII.2). Bacillariophyceae.

(b)   Frustules not swollen at each end, colonies either stellate or zig-zag **75**

75. (a)   Frustules with neither internal septa nor costae .... **Synedra** (in part see 160). **Synedra** has elongate, linear isopolar valves. There is a narrow pseudoraphe usually present. Fine transverse striae. Frustules single, short chains, stellate colonies or attached epiphytes. Wide-spread distribution and often abundant. Difficulties can be encountered with cleaned material in separating **Synedra** and **Fragilaria** as single cells. Bacillariophyceae.

(b)   Frustules with either internal septa or internal costae **76**

76. (a)   Frustules with internal longitudinal septa but no costae. Small polar and larger central swellings when seen from valve view .... **Tabellaria** (in part see 28). NB. Although swollen in valve view in girdle view, which is often the way in which they are seen if the colony is stellate or zig-zag, these swollen areas are not seen.

(b)   Frustules without internal septa but with thick internal costae. Valve ends often swollen but no median swelling – at most elliptical in valve view . **Diatoma** (in part see 28).

77. (a)   Cells elongate, cigar shaped arranged radially attached to each other at one end only. .... **Actinastrum** Cells of **Actinastrum** form small star-shaped colonies. The cigar-shaped cells have a single chloroplast with pyrenoid

and are 10–25μm long, 3–6μm broad. **A.hantzschii** is the commonest species and may be abundant in the plankton of lakes and rivers (Plate XIII.3). Chlorophyceae.

77. (b) Cells not greatly elongate, often spherical, cubical, crescent shaped or at the most short cylinders. Do not form star-shaped colonies. **78**

78. (a) Cells of colonies arranged within a definite mucilaginous envelope **79**

(b) Cells not within a definite mucilaginous envelope **87**

79. (a) Cells crescent-shaped or fusiform **80**

(b) Cells spherical, ovoid or other shape **81**

80. (a) Cells crescent-shaped, irregularly arranged in small mucilaginous colonies .... **Kirchneriella**
Kirchneriella cells have a parietal chloroplast with a pyrenoid. Cells are often so bent that the ends almost touch. Two common species are **K.lunaris** which has cells with pointed ends and **K.obesa** which has more bluntly rounded ends. **K.lunaris** cells are 3–8μm broad and 6–18μm long. It has up to 16 cells in a colony and is common in the plankton. **K.obesa** cells are 4–6μm broad and 10–14μm long and are also widely distributed. (Plate XIII.4). Chlorophyceae.

(b) Cells fusiform or wedge shaped ovals .... **Elakatothrix**
Cells of **Elakatothrix** are characteristically shaped and normally arranged in pairs within mucilaginous colonies. Chloroplast parietal with or without pyrenoid. Cells 3–6μm broad, 15–25μm in length. **E.gelatinosa** is an occasional planktonic species. (Plate XIII.5). Chlorophyceae.

81. (a) Cells spherical, ovoid or ellipsoidal, more or less radially arranged at the ends of strands and embedded in mucilage .... **Dictyosphaerium**
Cells of **Dictyosphaerium** are spherical to subreniform connected by threads (remnants of old mother-cell walls) and embedded in mucilage to form roundish colonies. Cells 3–10μm in diameter, parietal chloroplast with pyrenoid. Occurs frequently in the plankton of lakes and ponds. **D.ehrenbergianum** and **D.pulchellum** are common species. (Plate XIII.6). Chlorophyceae.

(b) Cells not radially arranged on the ends of strands embedded in mucilage **82**

82. (a) Cells of colony very densely packed often appearing dark brown to black in colour. Individual cells can be difficult to distinguish. .... **Botryococcus**
Cells of **Botryococcus** are difficult to see because they are

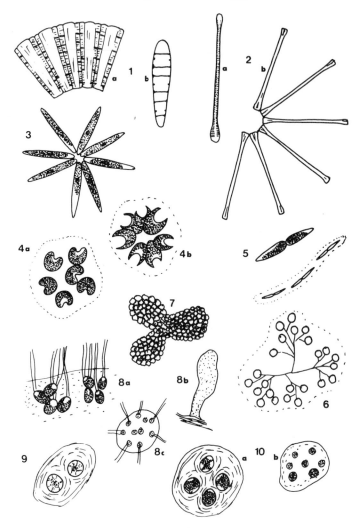

Plate XIII. 1. Meridion circulare; (a) colony, (b) cell. 2. Asterionella formosa; (a) cell, (b) colony. 3. Actinastrum hantzschii. 4. Kirchneriella; (a) K.lunaris, (b) K.obesa. 5. Elakatothrix gelatinosa. 6. Dictyosphaerium. 7. Botryococcus braunii. 8. Tetraspora geletinosa; (a) cells, (b) colony, (c) T.lacustris. 9. Asterococcus. 10. Gloeocystis; (a) G.gigas, (b) G.vesiculosa.

so densely packed and the colonies are so dark. They are spherical to angular in shape 3–9μm broad, 6–10μm long with a parietal chloroplast and pyrenoid. The cells are embedded in a tough oily mucilage which is usually brown in colour. **B.braunii** is the commonest species and is widespread in the plankton where it can be mistaken for particles of organic matter. (Plate XIII.7). Chlorophyceae.

82. (b)   Cells of colony not so densely packed and colonies not dark brown in colour **83**

83. (a)   Cells with pseudocilia .... **Tetraspora**
Tetraspora forms large irregular gelatinous colonies. Cells in groups of 2 or 4 within mucilage. Each cell normally has two fine pseudocilia and occur mostly around the edge of the colony. Chloroplast cup-shaped, pyrenoid present. Two common species are **T.gelatinosa** in which the colony is irregular, cells spherical 6–12μm wide and the pseudocilia are not always obvious (Plate XIII.8) and **T.lacustris** which has smaller colonies of spherical cells (7–10μm diameter) in which the long pseudocilia are more prominent. It is common in the plankton (Plate XIII.8). Chlorophyceae.

(b)   Cells without pseudocilia **84**

84. (a)   Mucilaginous surrounds to cells showing marked stratification or layering **85**

(b)   Mucilaginous surrounds to cells more or less homogenous, not markedly stratified **86**

85. (a)   Chloroplast dense and star-shaped. .... **Asterococcus**
Cells of **Asterococcus** are spherical, up to 40μm diameter. A central pyrenoid is normally present. Broad stratified or lamellate mucilage surrounds small groups of cells (4–8). Common in softer waters amongst other algae and moss (Plate XIII.9). Chlorophyceae.

(b)   Chloroplast cup shape although often fills the entire cell . ... **Gloeocystis**
Cells of **Gloeocystis** are spherical and usually grouped in 4–8–16 cells colonies surrounded by stratified or lamellate mucilage. There is a single pyrenoid and often many starch grains. The two commonest British species are **G.vesiculosa** which forms larger colonies of cells 4–12μm wide and is found in stagnant ponds and **G.gigas** which forms colonies of fewer cells each 9–17μm broad and are also found in stagnant waters. (Plate XIII.10). Chlorophyceae.

86. (a)   Chloroplast cup shaped with single pyrenoid. ... **Palmella**
Palmella has cells which are spherical, spheroidal or

rounded cylinders, 3–15μm broad. They are surrounded by an indefinite gelatinous mass. Forms green to reddish gelatinous masses on damp substrates and vegetation. Some other species of algae have palmelloid stages in their life-cycle giving rise to considerable confusion in this group. It is, for example, very similar to the non-motile stage of **Chlamydonomas** which has been observed to occur in slow-sand filters of waterworks, when prechlorination has been used, causing filter blocking. (Plate XIV.1). Chlorophyceae.

86. (b) Chloroplast parietal with 0 to many pyrenoids. .... **Sphaerocystis** Cells 7–20μm broad spherical. Colonies globular free floating with cells embedded in structureless mucilage. Reproduction is by a parent cell dividing to form 8–16μm densely packed daughter cells forming characteristic microcolonies within the parent colony. Common and sometimes abundant in the plankton of lakes, especially those with moderate to high enrichment. (Plate XIV.2). Chlorophyceae.

87. (a) Colonies either spherical, oval or a flat disc. **88**

(b) Colonies not as above **97**

88. (a) Cells of colony forming a flat disc **89**

(b) Cells forming a spherical or ovoid colony or globular groups of 4–16 cells **92**

89. (a) Colony or coenobium free floating .... **Pediastrum** **Pediastrum** forms flat disc-shaped colonies which are common in lakes, ponds and slow rivers specially where enrichment has occurred. The walls of the cells are tough and often persist for some time after the contents have died. There are a large number of species some of which are mentioned below. Chlorophyceae.

i(a) Colonies with distinct perforations or gaps (between cells .... **(ii)**

(b) Colony with no perforations or at the most minute interstices .... **(iii)**

ii(a) Edge cells with single spine or process. ..... **P.clathratum** Colonies or coenobia of **P.clathratum** are distinctive (Plate XIV.3) with the single spined marginal cells but they are relatively uncommon.

(b) Edge cells with double spines or processes. ...... **P.duplex** Colonies with 16–128 cells, the marginal ones of which are bilobed. Widely distributed (Plate XIV.4).

(iii)(a) Edge cells with single spine, lobe or process. . **P.simplex** **P.simplex** forms compact plates with single lobed margins but is uncommon. (Plate XIV.5).

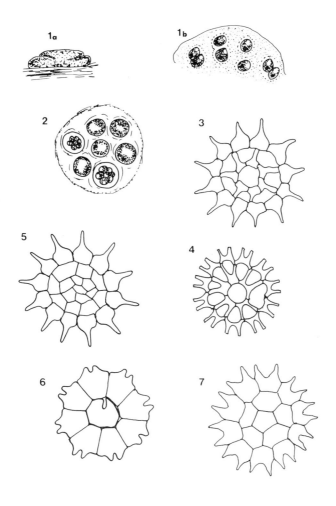

Plate XIV. 1. Palmella; (a) colony, (b) detail of cells. 2. Sphaerocystis. 3. Pediastrum clathratum. 4. P.duplex. 5. P.simplex. 6. P.tetras. 7. P.boryanum.

(iii)(b)   Edge cells with two spines, lobes or processes. .... **(iv)**

(iv)(a)   Colonies or coenobia of 4–8 cells, lobes or processes on outer cells small and the incision between the lobes narrow .... **P.tetras**
Coenobia of **P.tetras** are small, cells up to 16μm diameter. 4–celled colonies have a cross like appearance. Common and widely distributed (Plate XIV.6).

(b)   Colonies or coenobia up to 36 cells. Edge cells with two lobes or processes which are short and rounded. Gap or incision between lobes wide. .... **P.boryanum**
Cells up to 14μm diameter, 5–6 sided. Colonies can be large (up to 200μm). Common and widely distributed. (Plate XV.4).

89. (b)   Colony attached **90**

90. (a)   At least some cells bearing setae **91**

(b)   Cells without setae .... **Protoderma**
Protoderma forms a cushion or disc one cell thick (may become thicker with age) which is actually composed of irregularly branched filaments. The filamentous structure may become more obvious towards the disc edge. Cells quadrate to cyclindrical up to 15μm in length. Chloroplasts parietal with pyrenoid. **P.viride** is commonly attached to submerged aquatics. (Plate XV.1). Chlorophyceae.

91. (a)   Setae with sheaths, cells up to 40μm long. ....
.... **Coleochaetae (see 12)**

(b)   Setae not sheathed, frequent, cells up to 30μm long ....
.... **Chaetopeltis**
Colonies composed of radiating rectangular cells forming a flat disc (up to 1mm wide) on submerged aquatics. Chloroplast cup shaped. (Plate XV.2).

92. (a)   Cells bearing long spines and forming free Xfloating colonies .... **Micractinium**
Cells more or less spherical, 3–7μm in diameter, forming small colonies of usually 4 but up to 16 cells. Each cell with 1 to 5 fine tapering spines which are 10–35μm long. Chloroplasts parietal with single pyrenoid. **M.pusillum** is the commonest British species and occurs frequently (sometimes abundantly) in lakes, ponds and rivers – especially where the waters are eutrophic. (Plate XV.3). Chlorophyceae.

(b)   Cells without spines **93**

93. (a)   Cells globose to spherical, forming tightly packed hollow sphere of up to 100 cells **94**

(b)   Cells oval or with finger like processes extending outwards, more loosely arranged. Oval cells may have thickened poles or may be within an encasing envelope **95**

94. (a) Up to 100 cells per colony, loosely held together by the mother cell walls from the previous generation . **Westella**
Cells of **Westella** form a free-floating colony loosely connected by the original mother-cell walls. Cells 3–9µm diameter, chloroplast parietal, pyrenoid may be present. Planktonic. Regarded by some as synonymous with **Dictyosphaerium**. (Plate XV.4). Chlorophyceae.

(b) Hollow spherical colonies of up to 64 closely joined cells arranged regularly. .... **Coelastrum**
Cells of **Coelastrum** are spherical, 8–30µm in diameter, with a parietal chloroplast and a pyrenoid. Found in lakes and lake margins and in the plankton of eutrophic lakes and slow flowing rivers. Two species are common. (**C.microporum** has smooth walled cells joined by scarcely visible gelatinous threads (Plate XV.5). **C.cambricum** has cells with short truncated projections on the outer surface. Cells of colony joined to give more or less triangular intercellular spaces. (Plate XV.5). Chlorophyceae.

95. (a) Cells with finger or spine like processes extending outwards (1 to 4 per cell). Cells kidney shaped joined to each other by a mucilaginous protrubance so as to form a radiating colony .... **Sorastrum**
Sorastrum is related to **Pediastrum** but the cells form a more spherical colony of commonly 8–16–64 cells. Chloroplast parietal with pyrenoid. Outer facing surface of cell bears 1–4 finger or spine-like processes 4–15µm long. Cells 8–25µm long. Uncommon, found in similar locations to **Pediastrum**. (Plate XV.6). Chlorophyceae.

(b) Cells ovoid to spherical no spines or finger like processes
.... **96**

96. (a) Cells usually oval often with a clearly observable polar nodule at each end. Cell mother wall more or less entire and surrounds 2–4–8 daughter cells. Cells 4–50µm long. ..
.... **Oocystis** (in part see 171).

(b) Cells normally spherical without polar nodules. Cell mother walls fragmented, up to 10 cells per colony. Cells 3–9µm broad .... **Westella** (in part see 94)

97. (a) Cells roughly cylindrical (or sausage shaped, ellipsoidal or fusiform), usually more than 2 × lab. Colonies of usually single but sometimes double rows of 4–16 cells where cells join along the long axis .... **Scenedesmus**
Scenedesmus is a very common and sometimes abundant genus especially in eutrophic and hypertrophic waters.

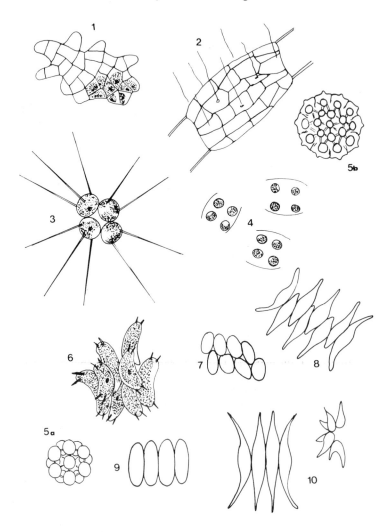

Plate XV. 1. Protoderma viride. 2. Chaetopeltis. 3. Micractinium pusillum. 4. Westella. 5. Coelastrum; (a) C.microporum, (b) C.cambricum. 6. Sorastrum. 7. Scenedesmus arcuatus. 8. S.acutus. 9. S.obliquus. 10. S.acuminatus.

Some species bear spines, others ridges and others no ornamentation. The species are variable but the commonest types are indicated below.

(i)(a)   Cell walls smooth, without spines ridges or warts ..... **(ii)**

(b)   Cell walls with ornamentation of either warts, spines or ridges .... **(vi)**

(ii)(a)   Cells fusiform with acute apices. Cells sometimes straight but often curved .... **(iii)**

(b)   Cells oval to bean shaped, 3–9μm wide, 6–17μm long. Often arranged in double or alternating series .... **S.arcuatus** (Plate XV.7).

(iii)(a)   All cells of colony same shape .... **(iv)**

(b)   End cells of colony different shape .... **(v)**

(iv)(a)   Cells in alternating series .... **S.acutus** (Plate XV.8)

(b)   Cells in linear series .... **S.obliquus** (Plate XV.9)

(v)(a)   Cells at end strongly arcuate, cells of colony do not lie in same plane .... **S.acuminatus** Cells of colony form a curved series (see Plate XV.10) with pointed apices.

(b)   Central cells fusiform, end cells crescent-shaped .... **S.dimorphus** (Plate XVI.1).

(vi)(a)   Cells having both spines and ridges. .... **S.armatus** Central cells of colony have longitudinal ridges (careful observation is sometimes needed to see them) end cells have two spines and a ridge. (Plate XVI.2).

(b)   cells without ridges .... **(vii)**

(vii)(a)   Cells with two (rarely 1) short tooth like spines at end .... **S.denticulatus** (Plate XVI.3).

(b)   Cells with at least two longer (5–15μm) spines .... **(viii)**

(viii)(a)   Cells with two prominant spines on outer cells, one spine at each end. .... **S.quadricauda** (Plate XVI.4).

(b)   Cells with spines at apices of each end cell and also 1 or more arising from face of end cells and possibly apices of middle cells. .... **S.abundans** (Plate XVI.5)

97. (b)   Cells as long as broad or spherical or very short cylinders joined end to end **98**

98. (a)   Cells very short cylinders (2–6μm broad 3–20μm long) joined end to end in 2s, 3s, 4s etc. .... **Stichococcus** (in part see 33).

(b)   Cells as long as broad, spherical or globose in shape . **99**

99. (a)   Cells with spines or projections **100**

(b)   Cells without spines or projections **101**

100. (a)   Cells spherical in groups of 4 (sometimes 2–16) each bearing one to five long tapering spines (many times as long as cell). .... **Micractinium** (in part see 92)

100. (b)   Cells angular in groups of four (may be solitary) spines usually very fine and shorter (not more than 2 cell diameter .... **Tetrastrum** Cells 3–7μm broad (excluding spines). Chloroplast cup shaped with or without pyrenoid. Commonest species **T.staurogeniaeforme** which occurs in the plankton but is not usually abundant (Plate XVI.6). Chlorophyceae.

101. (a)   Cells growing of moist substrate (e.g. treetrunks) – aerial. Cells globular or angular where touching forming definite clusters. .... **Pleurococcus** Isolated cells of **Pleurococcus** are globular but when in groups adjacent cell walls tend to get compressed. Chloroplast parietal usually with one small pyrenoid. Cells 5–20μm broad. Occurs as a characteristic covering of moist soils, treetrunks and posts. (Plate XVI.7). Chlorophyceae.

(b)   Cells aquatic, oval or triangular in shape, usually in groups of four often adhering together by means of a thin mucilaginous surround. .... **Crucigenia** Colonies of **Crucigenia** consist of four cells arranged in a cross so that a gap may be present at the colony centre. Cells have a parietal chloroplast and a small pyrenoid. Cells 5–10μm broad. **Crucigenia** is not uncommon in the plankton. Two common species are **C.tetrapedia** which has triangular cells arranged in fours with a small central space and **C.rectangularis** in which the cells are more ovate and have a larger central space. (Plate XVI.8). The genus is similar to **Tetrastrum** but has no spine.

102. (a)   Cells with flagella motile **103**
(b)   Cells without flagella non-motile **122**
N.B. Many pennate diatoms are capable of active gliding movements but do not have flagella. These are included in key number 140.

103. (a)   Cells covered with scales bearing long bristles or spines which superficially resemble flagella. One single apical flagellum used for locomotion. .... **Mallomonas** Cells of **Mallomonas** are an elongated oval shape and are covered with numerous overlapping silica plates which bear spines either over part or all of the body. The spines may become detached from the cells, especially on preservation. Two (common species are **M.acaroides** whose cells are about or less than × 2 lab (cells 7–20μm wide 8–25μm long) narrowing towards the anterior end and with spines mostly pointing backwards and having recurved tips and **M.caudata** whose cells are more than ×

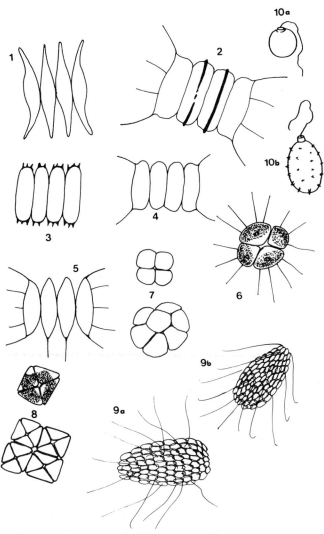

**Plate XVI. 1. Scenedesmus dimorphus. 2. S.armatus. 3. S.denticula-
tus. 4. S.quadricauda. 5. S.abundans. 6. Tetrastrum staurogeniae-
forme. 7. Pleurococcus. 8. Crucigenia tetrapedia. 9. Mallomonas;
(a) M.acaroides, (b) M.caudata. 10. Trachelomonas; (a) T.hispida,
(b) T.volvocina**

2 lab and tend to narrow towards the posterior end. The spines tend to point at all angles and do not have curved tips (cells 12–30μm wide 40–85μm long). Cells of both species have 1–2 parietal chloroplasts. They both occur in the plankton, sometimes in large numbers. They produce cysts which are spherical. (Plate XVI.9). Chrysophyceae.

103. (b)   Cells without spine bearing scales **104**

104. (a)   Cells with one, two or four flagella attached at anterior end only **105**

(b)   Cells with two flagella attached other than at anterior end **119**

105. (a)   Cells with a single emergent flagellum **106**

(b)   Cells with two or more emergent flagella **110**

106. (a)   Cells enclosed in a brownish test of various shapes with the flagellum emerging from an anterior aperture ....
.... **Trachelomonas**
Cells of **Trachelomonas** are enclosed in a roundish test or theca which may range in colour from pale to dark brown and is usually opaque. The test may be smooth, granulate or spiney. The single flagellum emerges from the anterior end through a round aperture. The chloroplasts, if visible, are few to numerous and disc shaped. A red eyespot is present. Most species occur in shallow waters, ditches small ponds etc. **T.volvocina** has a test 7–20μm in diameter which is smooth and does not have a collar where the flagellum emerges. It is common and widely distributed. **T.hispida** has a more oval test 15–26μm broad and 20–40μm long. There is a short raised collar where the flagellum emerges. The test is covered with short spines. Widely distributed but less common. (Plate XVI.10). Euglenophyceae.

(b)   Cells not enclosed in test **107**

107. (a)   Cells with pronounced dorsoventral flattening (leaf like in shape) often with some part of cell twisted .... **Phacus**
Cells of **Phacus** are markedly flattened, broad at the anterior end but pointed at the posterior. There are numerous small disc shaped chloroplasts. Common in similar habitats to **Euglena** in farm-yard ponds, with rotting vegetation or in the plankton. Three of the commoner species are listed below. Euglenophyceae.

(i)(a)   Tail straight, as long as, or longer than, body ....
.... **Phacus longicauda**
Cell oval, tapering to a long straight tail. Periplast striated. Paramylon body a circular plate. Cells 45–70μm broad, 80–170μm long. (Plate XVII.1).

(i)(b) Tail much shorter than cell body .... **(ii)**

(ii)(a) Cells small (less than 30μm in diameter) tail straight ......
.... **Phacus caudatus**
Cells ovoid with a spiral twist. Single large paramylon body, periplast striated. Cells 15–27μm broad, 30–50μm long. (Plate XVII.2).

(b) Cells large (greater than 30μm in diameter), tail curved obliquely to one side. .... **Phacus pleuronectes**
Cells ovoid with slight spiral. 1–2 paramylon bodies, periplast striated. Cells 37–50μm diameter, 50–80μm long. (Plate XVII.3)

107. (b) Cells not flattened or leaf like **108**

108. (a) Cells cylindrical or fusiform often metabolic (see glossary)
.... **Euglena**
Cells usually fusiform with one to many variously shaped chloroplasts. There is an apical reservoir from which a single flagellum emerges. A prominant eyespot (or stigma) can usually be seen as can one or more contractile vacuoles near to the reservoir. Storage granules of paramylon numerous and of various shapes. Common to abundant in small ponds. Euglenophyceae. The commoner species are listed below:

(i)(a) Chloroplasts small, numerous, discoid, pyrenoids absent .
.... **ii**

(b) Chloroplasts large, less numerous, usually with pyrnoid . **iv**

(ii)(a) Cell non-rigid exhibiting small to large amounts of euglenoid movement. Cell end (away from flagellum) rounded, paramylon in small granules. ..... **E.ehrenbergii**
Cells of **E. ehrenbergii** are 100–400 μm long. Swim with flagellum directed backwards. Occurs in small water bodies (even hoof marks) especially if enriched. Common but not in large numbers (Plate XVII.6).

(b) Cells almost completely rigid. Cell end with spine or tapering to fine point. Paramylon granules large doughnut shaped or rod shaped .... **iii**

(iii)(a) Cells elongate, fusiform, Paramylon granules rod shaped
.... **E.acus**
E.acus is common in the plankton of more acid waters (pH as low as 4.0). Plate XVII.5 Cells 80–150μm long.

(b) Cells more cylindrical, paramylon in two doughnut shaped bodies above and below nucleus.
E.spirogyra
E.spirogyra occurs in ditches especially when iron rich. Pellicle with spiral striations. 45–250μm long. Plate XVII.4.

(iv)(a)   Chloroplast in the shape of ribbons radiating from center of cell where small paramylon granules occur ... **E.viridis** **E.viridis** has cells up to 60μm in length which are broadly fusiform and none rigid. Paramylon granules small with no pyrenoid. Common in polluted waters often making pools look bright green. Plate XVII.9.

(b)   Chloroplasts other shape v

(v)(a)   Chloroplasts medium sized, flat, with marked pyrenoid (not covered with paramylon). Flagellum short – sometimes missing .... **E.mutabilis** **E.mutabilis** has a very short flagellum which is sometimes missing in which case movement is by creeping. Cell movement pronounced – by coiling. Found in acid muddy habitats. Length 50–150μm long. Plate XVII.10.

(b)   Chloroplasts large, pyrenoid with paramylon sheath. Obvious emergent flagellum **6**

(vi)(a)   Chloroplasts large flat shield shape 6–12 per cell with paramylon coated pyrenoid at centre. None rigid cell wall. .... **E.gracilis** **E.gracilis** swims rapidly and can show euglenoid movement. Often found amongst rotting leaves in ditches. Plate XVII.7.

(b)   Chloroplasts 2 per cell, side by side, with paramylon coated pyrenoid .... **E.pisciformis** The shape of **E.pisciformis** is variable. Swimming is rapid. Common in freshwaters. Plate XVII.8

108. (b)   Cells ovoid to pyriform not metabolic **109**

109. (a)   Cells ovoid, periplast firm with pointed tail ... **Lepocinclis** **Lepocinclis** is found in similar, but slightly less rich waters, than **Euglena**. Cells circular in section, periplast spirally straited. Chloroplasts numerous discoid, eye-spot anterior; 2 annular paramylon granules. Cells 10–20μm broad, 25–40μm long. (Plate XVIII.1). Euglenophyceae.

(b)   Cells oval, mildly metabolic, no tail. .... **Chromulina** Widespread in cleaner waters usually amongst vegetation. Cells ovoid with one curved platelike or two chloroplasts, and with leucosin mass at posterior of cell, whitish in colour. Cells 6–7μm broad, 9–14μm long. (Plate XVIII.2). Chrysophyceae.

110. (a)   Cells having 4 flagella **111**

(b)   Cells having 2 flagella **113**

111. (a)   Cells with a broad crescent shape.) .... **Spermatozopsis** **Spermatozopsis exsultans** although not usually abundant, has been recorded from a number of locations, usually from still waters. Cells are roughly crescent-shaped with a

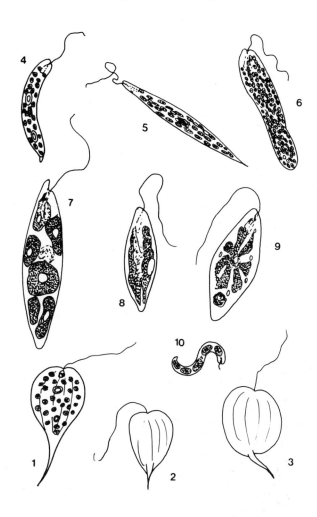

Plate XVII. 1. Phacus longicauda. 2. P.caudatus. 3. P.pleuronectes.
4. Euglena spirogyra. 5. E.acus. 6. E.eherenbergii. 7. E.gracilis.
8. E.pisciformis. 9. E.viridis. 10. E.mutabilis.

	broad central region. Four flagella arise from the anterior end. Cells 9–12μm long, 3–4μm broad. (Plate XVIII.3). Chlorophyceae.
111. (b)	Cells ovoid, perhaps with a truncated anterior end ... **112**
112. (a)	Cell strawberry-shaped, 4–lobed, forming indentation at anterior end from which flagella arise ...... **Pyramimonas** The cells are a characteristic strawberry or subpyramidal shape. Chloroplast cup-shaped and often 4-lobed towards the front. Cells naked, without wall, 12–16μm broad, 20–30μm long. Widespread in ponds and still waters often at colder times of the year. (Plate XVIII.4). Chlorophyceae.
(b)	Cells oval or occasionally heart-shaped but not lobed .... **Carteria** Cells of **Carteria** are virtually the same as those of **Chlamydomonas** except for the possession of 4 flagella instead of 2. Frequent, occasionally abundant in still waters. Cells 9–20μm in diameter. Less common than **Chlamydomonas.** (Plate XVIII.5). Chlorophyceae.
113. (a)	Cells fusiform .... **Chlorogonium** Cells of **Chlorogonium** are fusiform or spindleshaped with two flagella arising from a narrow front end. It has a rigid cell wall. Chloroplast fills most of cell and pyrenoids are present. Cells 5–12μm broad and up to 50μlong. Can occur in large numbers in smaller water bodies. (Plate XVIII.6). Chlorophyceae.
(b)	Cells not fusiform **114**
114. (a)	Cells with anterior end flattened obliquely (in one view). Flagella inserted obliquely near to front end and of slightly unequal length. **115**
(b)	Cells with anterior end rounded or flattened transversely. Flagella inserted apically and of equal length **117**
115. (a)	Cells obovoid but strongly curved so that one side is strongly convex and the other almost concave; hyaline tail present .... **Rhodomonas** **Rhodomonas** cells are small (8–15μm long) and fairly delicate so, although it is common and widely distributed, it is often overlooked. No obvious gullet is present and the cells are not metabolic. A large pyrenoid is present along one side with a definite starch sheath. Hyaline tail with basal granule present. Commonest species **R.minuta.** (Plate XVIII.7). Cryptophyceae.
115. (b)	Cells not strongly curved; tail, if present, not hyaline **116**

116. (a)   Gullet absent, chloroplast blue to blue-green or reddish ..
.... **Chroomonas**
Cells of **Chroomonas** and **Cryptomonas** (116b) are very
similar except in colour of chloroplast, the absence of a
gullet and are usually smaller. Although a furrow may be
present at the anterior and in **Chroomonas** this is not
extended into a gullet. Occurs in ponds and shallow
waters. Starch stored. Cells 9–16μm long. (Plate XVIII.8).
Cryptophyceae.

(b)   Gullet present, chloroplasts brown to olive green ....
.... **Cryptomonas**
Cells of **Cryptomonas** are slipper to bean-shaped flattened
dorsiventrally, gullet more conspicuous as a longitudinal
furrow extending inwards from the anterior end. One or
2 chloroplasts which are arranged laterally and may have
pyrenoids. Olive brown in colour. Storage product starch.
Widespread in distribution in small to moderate numbers
especially in organically enriched waters. **Cryptomonas
ovata** has larger cells (up to 80μm long) with a long gullet
(up to 3/4 cell length) and no pyrenoid. **C.erosa** is smaller
($<$ 32μm long) with a shorter gullet ($< \frac{1}{2}$ length of cell).
C.tetrapyrenoidosa has four conspicuous large pyrenoids
(cells 20–50μm long) and is less common. (Plate XVIII.9
to 11). Cryptophyceae.

117. (a)   Chloroplast in centre of cell and connected to cell wall by
strands of cytoplasm.
.... **Haematococcus**
Cells of **Haematococcus** (sometimes called **Sphaerella**) are
oval, 8–30μm in diameter. The green pigments are often
masked by the red hhaematochrome. **H.lacustris** is the
common form often occurring in bird baths, manhole
covers, etc., giving them a red appearance. (Plate XIX.1).
Chlorophyceae.

(b)   Chromatophore not attached to cell wall with cytoplasmic
strands **118**

118. (a)   Cells with hyaline wing along either side. ...... **Pteromonas**
Cells of **Pteromonas** are compressed laterally with a
bivalved envelope which extends into a wing along either
side of the cell. Pyrenoids present. **P.angulosa** is the most
common species having cells 15–17μm long and 14–17μm
broad. Found in ponds and relatively still waters. (Plate
XIX.2). Chlorophyceae.

(b)   Cells without hyaline wing .... **Chlamydomonas.**
There are a very large number of species of **Chlamydomonas** described but many are probably not true species.

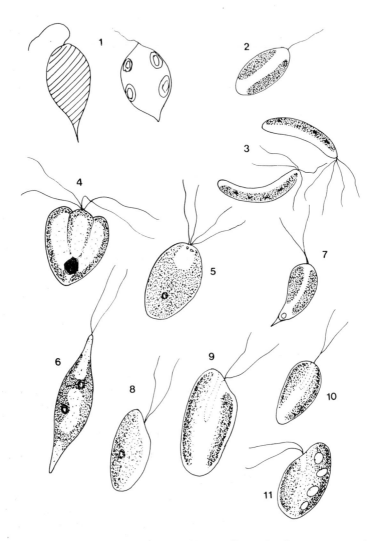

Plate XVIII. 1. Lepocinclis. 2. Chromulina. 3. Spermatozopsis exsultans. 4. Pyramimonas. 5. Carteria. 6. Chlorogonium. 7. Rhodomonas minuta. 8. Chroomonas. 9. Cryptomonas ovata. 10. C.erosa. 11. C.tetrapyrenoidosa.

Members of the genes are widely distributed occupying a large range of habitats where they may occasionally be abundant. Habitats range from water butts to ditches to temporary pools to lakes. Cells contain a large cup shaped (usually) chloroplast with a red coloured eye-spot or stigma. One or more pyrenoids may be present. When certain conditions prevail most species have the ability of coming to rest, shedding their flagella and secreting a mucilaginous surround. Vegetative division may continue producing an amorphous gelatinous mass or palmelloid stage. A selection of the commoner species is described below. **Dunaliella** is a closely related brackish water/marine species but differs in that it lacks a cell wall and may be metabolic. It can produce reddish blooms. Chlorophyceae.

(i)(a)   Chloroplast with more than one pyrenoid .... **(ii)**

(b)   Chloroplast with single pyrenoid .... **(iii)**

(ii)(a)   Chloroplast with 2 pyrenoids .... **C.platyrhyncha**
C.platyrhyncha has nearly spherical cells about $18-25\mu m$ long with a small rounded papilla or cell wall extension between the two flagella. Frequent but not abundant. Other members of the **Bicocca** and **Amphichloris** groups of Chlamydomonas would key out here although the latter have a more complex H shaped chloroplast. All are generally less common (Plate XIX.3).

(b)   Chloroplasts with 3 or more pyrenoids. .... **C.sphagnicola**
C.sphagnicola has 4–6 pyrenoids. Cells subspherical $25-35\mu m$ long with a double papilla between the flagella and a thicker gelatinous wall. (Plate XIX.4).

(iii)(a)   Cells ovoid, anterior end slightly truncate, definite papilla present .... **C.angulosa**
This species differs from **C.globosa** in having a papilla. Cells $11-15\mu m$ diameter, $15-20\mu m$ long. Eyespot present. Common and widespread. (Plate XIX.5).

(b)   Cells ovoid to globose, anterior end rounded with no papilla present .... **C.globosa**.
The cells of **C.globosa** are globose or broadly ovoid, $5-7\mu m$ in diameter and $10-19\mu m$ long. Eyespot and pyrenoid usually present. Common and widespread. (Plate XIX.6).

119. (a)   Cells with a long anterior horn and two or three posterior horns .... **Ceratium**.
Ceratium cells are large and brownish in colour. They possess one anterior process or horn and two or three posterior processes. There is a narrow but obvious transverse furrow across the middle of the cell which houses the transverse flagellum. There is a much more

shallow less obvious furrow leading downwards (the bottom being taken as the part with 2–3 horns) from a flatter area in the centre and housing the ventral flagellum. The body is covered by a specifically arranged series of plates which, when observed in dead cells or cell fragments, can be seen to be distinctly areolate. Cells overall are strongly flattened and may be curved if viewed from the end. Numerous small brown disc-shaped chloroplasts are present. Cysts are commonly produced at the end of the growing season (autumn). These are more compact (without the long horns) dense and thick walled often with some spiny processes.

This is quite a variable species. **Ceratium hirundinella** is the commonest fresh-water species usually having (but not always) three posterior horns. Cells vary in size but may be up to 400µm long. Widely distributed in the plankton of enriched eutrophic lakes where it may dominate and produce brown coloration. Because of its motility it can migrate vertically through the water column. It has been reported as imparting taste and odour to the water. **C.cornutum** is described as having a shorter apical horn (less than the length of the main cell) which is at an angle to the rest of the cell. It has a more massive body. (Plate XIX.7). Dinophyceae.

119. (b)	Cells otherwise shaped **120**
120. (a)	Cell wall thin and difficult to see except in empty cells, or completely absent **121**
(b)	Cell wall thick, plates easily seen, sutures between plates evident, transverse furrow encircling cell ...... **Peridinium**

For the proper identification of **Peridinium** species it is essential to be able to observe the number and arrangement of the armoured plates. These armoured plates are angular and cover the entire cell. Generally they are smooth but sometimes small groups of spines may be present. The transverse groove is slightly offset so that the upper part – the epicone – is of a slightly different size to the lower part – the hypocone. The epicone usually has about 13 plates and the hypocone about 7. Cells may be roughly globular in outline or slightly more elongate. They are common and may be abundant in the plankton. The most frequently occurring species are listed below. Resting cysts may be produced. Dinophyceae.

(i)(a) Cells small, 15–30µm long, with small pore present at apex of epicore .... **P.inconspicuum**.

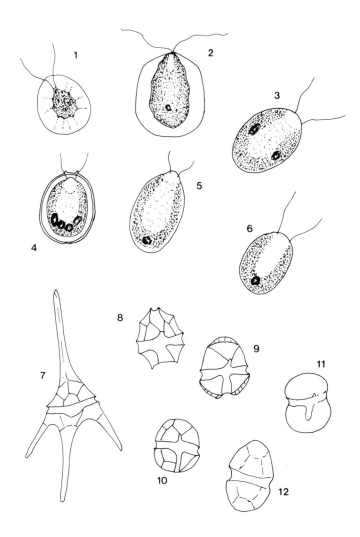

Plate XIX. 1. Haematococcus. 2. Pteromonas angulosa. 3. Chlamydomonas platyrhyncha. 4. C.sphagnicola. 5. C.angulosa. 6. C.globosa. 7. Ceratium hirundinella. 8. Peridinium inconspicuum. 9. P.willei. 10. P.cinctum. 11. Gymnodinium. 12. Glenodinium.

This species has small ovoid cells with a slightly pointed apical region. Plates difficult to see in live cells. Can occur in large numbers in softer waters (Plate XIX.8).

(i)(b)   Cells larger > 30µm, no apical pore .... **ii**

(ii)(a)   Cells more elongate (1 to 1.5 lab). Transverse furrow pronounced with raised edge .... **P.willei**.
Cells 45–70µm long but only 45–50µm wide. The cell wall has a winglike flange forming a crest anteriorly and two lobes posteriorly. Numerous disk-shaped brown chromatophores. Epithica with 7 precingular, 3 apical, 2 ventral apical, and one dorsal plate, and a rhomboidal plate; hypotheca with 5 postcingular and 2 large antapical plates. Slight dorso-ventral flattening. Common in plankton, ponds and ditches. (Plate XIX.9).

(b)   Transverse furrow broad without raised edges. Cells nearly circular in outline, globose. .. **Peridinium cinctum**
Cell of **P. cinctum** are nearly round, not much longer than broad (30–55µm broad, 40–60µm long). Numerous brown disk-shaped chromatophores. Epithica of 4 apical (including rhomboidal plate), 3 intercalary and 7 precingular plates, hypotheca with 5 postcingular, 2 antapical plates. Slight dorsoventral flattening. Common in ponds, ditches and plankton. (Plate XIX.10).

121. (a)   Cells without walls, protoplast naked ...... **Gymnodinium**
Cells roughly oval in outline but with no cell wall. Slight central furrow around which is found one flagellum, with a second trailing backwards. Numerous golden-brown chromatophores. General shape of organism gives impression of a helmet. They may be abundant but are most frequently found in small bodies of stagnant water. Cells 30–100 µm long. (Plate XIX.11). Dinophyceae.

(b)   Cells with thin walls of plates which may be difficult to see except in empty cells. .... **Glenodinium**
Cells with firm but delicate wall, poles more rounded than in **Peridinium**. Common but not abundant. Cells 20–40µm broad, globose in shape. Theca very thin with faintly marked plates. Chromatophores numerous, brown, oval in shape. Pigment spot usually present. Resting cysts may be produced. (Plate XIX.12). Dinophyceae.

122. (a)   Cells isolated or in groups, wall siliceous and etched with grooves or dots (punctae) forming a definite pattern. Storage products mainly oil, and droplets may be visible in the cells. **123**

(b)   Cell wall not siliceous or decorated; no conspicuous oil droplets. **167**

74

123. (a)   Cells circular in outline in valve view, decorations arranged in radial rows, cells often solitary although they may sometimes adhere in loose chains **124**

(b)   Cells elongate, cigar-, boat-, or crescent-shaped; decorations arranged bilaterally. **133**
NB. The structure of the diaton cell wall is complex and some features may be difficult to see using light microscopy alone. In many cases scanning electron microscopy may be required for positive identification. It is realised that this facility will not be available to many users of this text. An attempt has thus been made to limit the features used to those which can be clearly seen by light microscopy but this is not always possible unless the best equipment is available. Readers are strongly recommended to consult the more detailed texts mentioned in the bibliography.

124. (a)   Valve with hyaline central area with 5–7 broad hyaline rays extending to valve margin. .... **Asteromphalus**
Asteromphalus is a widely distributed marine species which is common in cold temperate waters and can be found in estuarine samples. The valves are circular or flat. Between the hyaline rays are fine or coarse areolae depending on species. Cell diameter 25–100μm. Numerous discoid chloroplasts. (Plate XX.1). Bacillariophyceae.

(b)   Valve without broad hyaline rays **125**

125. (a)   Markings on valve surface divided into six (usually) distinct sectors that are alternately raised and lowered giving an alternating light and dark appearance ....
.... **Actinoptychus**
Actinoptychus is a cosmopolitan marine coastal and estuarine species common at most times of the year. The markings on the valve are characteristic. (Plate XX.2). The sectors are covered with coarse areolation. Chloroplasts plate like or irregular. Cells 20–80μm diameter. Bacillariophyceae.

(b)   Valve markings not divided into alternately raised and lowered sectors **126**

126. (a)   Margin or rim of valve with spines **127**
(NB. **Coscinodiscus** (132) may have spines but they are not usually visible).

(b)   No spines on rim or margin of valve **128**

127. (a)   Cells usually colonial joined by a mucous thread from the valve centre. Punctae in a radiating mesh-like pattern although sometimes in arcs. Valve surface virtually flat ...
.... **Thalassiosira**
Cells of **Thalassiosira** may be solitary but are frequently

75

joined to form loose chains. Valves circular with a flat face covered with fairly coarse punctae which may be radial or arranged in arcs. Small spines at valve margin. Chloroplasts small discs, numerous. Cells 15–40μm diameter. Very common and widely distributed in marine habitats and also common in estuaries. Can reach very large numbers in coastal waters. **T.fluviatilis** and **T.baltica** are frequently brackish water species. (Plate XX.3 and 4).

Bacillariophyceae.

127. (b) Cells usually solitary, occasionally colonial, valve surface with radiating rows of punctae (single towards centre sometimes double or more at edge). Central area punctate but rows not as clearly defined. Valve surface concentrically undulate .... **Stephanodiscus**
Cells of **Stephanodiscus** are disc or barrel shaped. Valve face undulate with either the centre raised or depressed compared with the margin. Valve surface covered with radiating rows of fine punctae almost reaching centre – central area has less well defined rows of punctae. Valve margin with a ring of short spines and, in some species, delicate organic threads which are quite long and radiate outwards. Chloroplasts discoid numerous. The taxonomy of Stephanodiscus has been subject of considerable discussion.

Species of Stephanodiscus are common in freshwater (some extending into brackish waters). These may be abundant, particularly in eutrophic waters where they may be used to indicate enrichment. Bacillariophyceae.

Because of the continuing problems with the taxonomy of this group it has been decided to substantially follow the description and nomenclature adopted by Round[13] in describing the commoner species.

(i)(a) Cells small < 30μm .... **(ii)**
(b) Cells larger > 30μm .... **(iii)**
(ii)(a) Valves 8–20μm diameter, weakly silicified so that markings are a little indistinct. Cells may be solitary or in short chains, barrel shaped. Long fine spines of organic material may be present at valve margin .... **S.hantzschii**
S.hantzschii is a common planktonic species of rivers and lakes especially where the waters are enriched. (Plate XX.5).
(b) Valves 8–30μm diameter, more strongly silicified. Rows of punctae/areolae single towards centre, 2–3 wide at margin. Small marginal spines occur at (end of hyaline

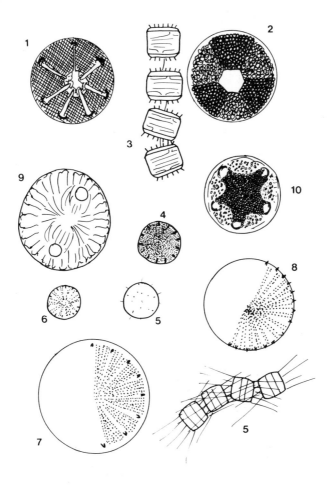

Plate XX. 1. Asteromphalus. 2. Actinoptychus. 3. Thalassiosira fluviatillis. 4. T.baltica. 5. Stephanodiscus hantzschii. 6. S.minutula. 7. S.niagarae. 8. S.rotula. 9.Auliscus. 10. Aulacodiscus.

rays .... **S.minutula**

S.minutula (referred to as **S.rotula var. minutula** by Hartley 1986) is usually solitary. Its valves have conspicuous raised or depressed central areas. Common in plankton of eutrophic lakes (Plate XX.6).

(iii)(a) Cells large (up to 89μm). Punctae/areolae up to 3 or 5 per row at valve margin .... **S.niagarae**

S.niagare is a large freshwater species which is well silicified. Valves shallow, saucer like, with slight undulations. Punctae/areolae single towards centre but double and 3–5 per row at margin. Spines sub-marginal. Cells 47–89 (−100)μm in diameter. (Plate XX.7).

(b) Cells 30–50μm diameter. Punctae/areolae in paired rows away from the centre along at least 1/2 the radius ....

.... **S.rotula**

S.rotula, which covers most (although not all) of the description of **S.astraea** is more heavily silicified than **S.minuta**. The punctae extend in rows over the valve edge to the mantle. Spines usually occur towards the end of the hyaline areas between the punctae although not each area has a spine. Very common in the plankton of eutrophic lakes. (Plate XX.8).

NB. All species of **Stephanodiscus** noted above have been recorded as causing problems at potable water treatment works mainly through blocking filters.

128. (a) Valve face with two or more processes or ocelli on surface, visible as obvious larger structures on surface ....

.... **129**

(b) No obvious larger structures on valve surface **130**

129. (a) Cells broadly elliptical or subcircular. Two large ocelli on surface of valve which is decorated with lines around margin and radiating from central area .... **Auliscus**

Auliscus cells are usually attached to sand, stones or rocks in the marine environment and are bottom living and so are only occasionally found in the plankton. They are common in coastal waters. Cells 40–80μm. The shape of the cell and the large ocelli are characteristic of the species. (Plate XX.9). Bacillariophyceae.

(b) Cells circular in valve view. Valve surface flat at centre but raised as it goes outwards towards the marginal processes. Processes may have furrow running back towards valve centre. Valve surface areolate ....

.... **Aulacodiscus**

A marine species associated with sediments where it can be very common. The processes on the valve surface are variable in number but normally range between 3 and 8. Cell diameter 60–200µm. (Plate XX.10). Bacillariophyceae.

130. (a)   Valve surface apparently mostly devoid of markings and with large concentric clear area around centre ....

.... **Hyalodiscus**
Hyalodiscus cells are either sessile, in short chains or as individuals in the marine plankton. Valves circular and strongly convex with the centres slightly flattened. Because of the markedly convex nature of the valve only a small part can be in focus at any one time using light microscopy, hence the apparent lack of markings. In fact the whole valve surface is covered with areolae arranged in radial rows. Chloroplasts numerous and rod shaped. Cells 12–115µm diameter. (Plate XXI.1). Bacillariophyceae.

(b)   Valve surface with markings over whole or most of surface **131**

131. (a)   Valve surface with two distinct areas of markings. Middle area punctate, outer area striate or ribbed ..... **Cyclotella**
Valves of **Cyclotella** are circular and usually slightly undulate. Valve margins without spines but in some species small tubules are present which might be mistaken as spines. The central area is irregularly punctate but the concentric outer area is regularly striate. Cells are usually solitary but may be attached in chains by mucilaginous threads. Very widespread in occurrence in lakes, rivers, marine and brackish water environments. Some of the commoner freshwater species are indicated below. Bacillariophyceae.

(i)(a)   Cells less than 10µm in diameter .... **(ii)**

(b)   Cells greater than 10µm in diameter .... **(iii)**

(ii)(a)   Central area feebly punctate, raised punctae forming a concentric circle amongst the marginal striations ....

.... **Cyclotella operculata**
Cells between 6 and 30µm diameter. Outer zone with fairly coarse striae (13–15 per 10µm); inner zone weakly punctate. Chromatophores goldenbrown. Common, widely distributed in the plankton, especially in slow flowing rivers. (Plate XXI.2).

(b)   Central area smooth or occasionally with a few delicate punctae or small striations at or near to the centre. No raised punctae amongst the radial striations ....

.... **Cyclotella glomerata**
Cells 4–10µm in diameter. Outer zone with radial striae (13–15 per 10µm), inner zone sometimes smooth and

sometimes with a ring of fine punctae or short striae in centre. Sometimes forming loose chains in which not all of the cells touch each other. Common in the plankton. (Plate XXI.3).

(iii)(a) Central area smooth .... **(iv)**

(b) Central area punctate .... **(v)**

(iv)(a) Marginal striae broad, 8–9 in 10μm. ....
.... **Cyclotella meneghiniana**
Cells 10–30μm in diameter with broad outer striae but smooth central area. Widely distributed and common. (Plate XXI.4).

(b) Marginal striae fine 12–14 in 10μm. ....
.... **Cyclotella kutzingiana**
Cells 10–45μm in diameter. Marginal striations finer than in **C.meneghiniana**. Common and widely distributed. The central area is usually smooth but it may occasionally show one or two fine punctae. (Plate XXI.5).

(v)(a) Cells 15–50μm in diameter, central area extending to half the radius. Fairly heavy radial striae 13–15 in 10μm, small, darker short striae between normal striae which form a concentric circle near to the margin ....
.... **Cyclotella compta**
Characterized by the presence of some shorter, darker striae amongst the others. Widely distributed and sometimes abundant in the plankton. (Plate XXI.6).

(b) Cells 6–30μm in diameter, central area not so large, radial striae delicate 13–15 in 10μm, concentric circle of raised punctae amongst the radial striae ....
.... **Cyclotella operculata See (ii)**

131. (b) Valve markings not with two distinct concentric areas ....
.... **132**

132. (a) Valve surface flat to slightly convex. Areolae in straight parallel rows of decreasing length giving the surface a segmented cross hatched appearance .... **Actinocyclus**
Valves of **Actinocyclus** are circular to slightly sub-circular. There is a small central hyaline area with irregular punctae. The valve face is marked with areolae in regular parallel rows of decreasing length. (see Plate XXI.7).
Chromatophores plate like, numerous. Cells 20–170μm diameter. Common in coastal plankton and as an epiphyte in marine waters. Bacillariophyceae.

(b) Valve surface gently undulate. Coarse markings (punctae/areolate) over surface forming radial rows or arcs. Areolae circular or hexagonal. .... **Coscinodiscus**
The valve markings on **Coscinodiscus** are generally coarse

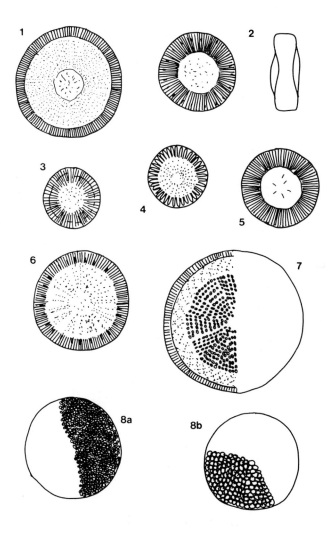

Plate XXI. 1. Hyalodiscus. 2. Cyclotella operaculata. 3. C.glomerata. 4. C.meneghiniana. 2. C.kutzingiana. 6. C.compta. 7. Actinocyclus. 8. Coscinodiscus lacustris.

and often hexagonal in shape although not always so. They cover the whole valve surface except for a small central hyaline area which may be present together with a rosette of larger areolae (although this may be present without the hyaline area). The valve margin may have small spines but these are seldom visible under light microscopy. Chloroplasts numerous and plate like. Free living abundant in plankton. Mostly marine, only on British freshwater species, **C.lacustris**. Cells up to 300µm in diameter.

(Plate XXI.8). Bacillariophyceae.

133. (a)   Cells very elongate, tubular, at least × 10 lab. No obvious raphe or pseudoraphe area. Ends taper to form one or two often short spines. Main body of cell with transverse markings which are sometimes difficult to see **134**

(b)   Cells not as long, or if long have a raphe or pseudoraphe present. Cell ends without spines. **135**

134. (a)   Valve end with one spine .... **Rhizosolenia**
Frustules of **Rhizosolenia** are elongate and cylindrical with the apices drawn out into either a long or, more frequently, a short spine. Cells are free-living or chain forming. Chloroplasts numerous plates. The valves are asymmetrical as the cone like shapes and spines point on opposite sides. The body of the cell is actually the girdle and is composed of many segments or plates giving rise to the transverse markings. A very common marine and brackish water genus with cells up to 1500µm in length and 100µm in diameter. The freshwater species, **R.eriensis**, found in the plankton of some larger lakes, has long tapering spines at each end rather than the short ones of marine species. Because of this, and other features Round (1990) places it in the genus **Urosolenia**. (Plate XXII.1). Bacillariophyceae.

(b)   Valve with two spines at each end .... **Attheya**
Frustules of **Attheya** are elongate and cylindrical. At the ends of the cell are two long spines, one at each side. The general structure is very delicate. The cell body, which is really the girdle area, has many transverse markings which, again, very fine. A planktonic species of nutrient rich waters. The only British species from freshwater is **A.zachariasi** which has now been placed in the genus **Acanthoceras**. Other true species of **Attheya** are coastal marine species. (Plate XXII.2).

135. (a)   Cells small, rectangular in girdle view, united in chains by means of long interlocking bristles or setae. Valves

elliptical and bristles arise at corners .... **Chaetoceros**
Cells of **Chaetoceros** are weakly silicified and delicate.
They may thus be destroyed by acid cleaning. This is a
very common marine planktonic species with numerous
representatives. Although rectangular in girdle view the
cells are elliptical in valve view. The valve margin is
usually upturned to produce a deep valve mantle. From
the valve apices arise two long bristles or setae. Those
from different cells interlock and may be fused to form
chains. Setae up to × 20 valve width. Cells 5–60µm in
diameter. (Plate XXII.3). Bacillariophyceae.

135. (b)   Cells not united in chains by means of long setae **136**

136. (a)   Cells approximately rectangular in girdle view with definite
large processes at the corners. Valves bipolar; triangular,
polyonal or ovoid in shape .... **Biddulphia**
Biddulphia cells often grow in chains or zig-zag colonies
in inshore waters. May be planktonic or an epiphyte.
Valve bipolar and often with wavy edges. Valve surface
coarsely areolate. Cells large – up to 300µm long.
Chloroplasts rounded, numerous. Many species are
common in the plankton of coastal waters. (Plate XXII.4).

(b)   Cells without large processes at corners **137**

137. (a)   Cells triangular with small swellings at corner. Valve
surface flat and covered with coarse circular to rectangular
areolae .... **Triceratium**
Triceratium is a common free living coastal and estuarine
planktonic form. The valve face is triangular with slightly
curved edges. The apices have definite swelling but much
smaller than in **Biddulphia**. The valve surface is covered
with a regular pattern of coarse areolae. Cells are oblong
in girdle view. Cells up to 100µm across the angles. (Plate
XXII.5). Bacillariophyceae.

(b)   Cells not triangular with growths at the corners. **138**

138. (a)   Cells ovate, egg shaped, cuneate in valve view. May be
twisted about the long (apical) axis. **139**

(b)   Cells elongate, lanceolate, sigmoid, lunate or shape other
than ovoid or egg shaped **140**

139. (a)   Cells flattened, symmetrically oval in outline (valve view).
Valve markings either fine or rarely coarse punctae in
rows.
Epiphytic .... **Cocconeis**
Valves of **Cocconeis** are isopolar and isobilateral but it is
heterovalvar, one valve having a pseudoraphe but the
other having a true raphe. Striae uniseriate run from
raphe/pseudoraphe to margin. Punctae often fine but may

be coarse. A very widespread and common genus occurring in all waters from marine to freshwater. All species are sessile and are common, sometimes abundant, epiphytes. The more abundant species are indicated below. Bacillariophyceae.

(i)(a) Punctae on valve coarse .... **C.scutellum**
Cocconeis scutellum is a common coastal marine and brackish water species. 45–60μm long 30–40μm wide. (Plate XXII.6).

(b) Punctae fine .... **ii**

(ii)(a) Valves rhomboidal to oval elliptical in outline, 15–56μm long, 10–37μm broad. .... **Cocconeis pediculus** Abundant as epiphytes on filamentous algae and other aquatic plants. No smooth, hyaline intermarginal zone present as in **C.placentula** (165(b)). Fine punctate striations almost radially arranged; 16–18 striations per 10μm, punctae 18–12 per 10μm. Frustule 10–37μm wide, 15–56μm long. Single mid-brown chromatophore with 1 or 2 pyrenoids. (Plate XXII.7).

(b) Valves elliptical, 11–70μm long, 8–40μm broad. ....
.... **Cocconeis placentula**
Distinguished from **C.pediculus** by its elliptical rather than rhomboid shape. An equally common epiphyte. Both species are less common in badly polluted waters. Striations on valve transverse, but sometimes radial 23–25 per 10μm. Intermarginal hyaline area present. Single mid-brown parietal chromatophore with 1 or 2 pyrenoids. (Plate XXII.8).

139. (b) Cells heteropolar or if isopolar an elongate oval with more pointed apices. Valves with prominent rib-like markings along the margins. Striae difficult to see with light microscopy. .... **Surirella** Cells of **Surirella** are solitary and cuneate in girdle view. In valve view they are mostly ovate to egg-shaped and heteropolar with the upper end broadly rounded and the lower end more sharply pointed. Rarely isopolar then usually with both ends broadly round or both more sharply pointed. Occasionally the cell may be constricted at the centre. The raphe system is around the margin and supported by raised ribs which give rise to the rib-like markings around the valve margin. There is generally a hyaline area along the apical axis down the valve centre. Either side of this may be seen fine striations in between rib-like extension of the raphe support system. A large and common freshwater to marine genus. Cells benthic,

84

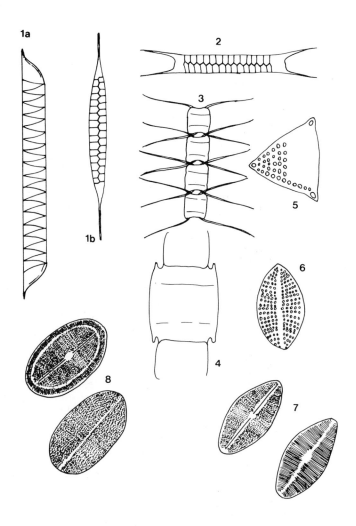

Plate XXII. 1. Rhizosolenia eriensis. 2. Attheya zachariasi. 3. Chaetoceros. 4. Biddulphia. 5. Triceratium. 6. Cocconeis scutellum. 7. C.pediculus. 8. C.placentula

rarely planktonic seldom abundant. Many species. Bacillariophyceae.

(i)(a) Cell symmetrical, isopolar, (both top and bottom ends
the same). 80–350μm long and 30–80μm broad. ....
.... **Surirela biseriata**
Common in the plankton. Distinguished by its symmetrical
valves which are lanceolate in shape. Valve sides parallel
or very slightly convex at central region; 1 or 2 costae per
10μm. Two chromatophores present, one along each
valve. Numerous pyrenoids. (Plate XXIII.1).

(b) Cells asymmetrical, heteropolar (bottom end narrower
than top) .... **ii**

(ii)(a) Cells small (20–100μm long, 10–40μm broad), fairly broad
in relation to length, bottom end fairly acutely pointed ...
.... **Surirella ovalis**
A fairly small but very abundant species. The narrow end
of the frustule is fairly sharply pointed as opposed to
rounded. Costae 4–5 per 10μm. Two chromatophores and
numerous pyrenoids present. (Plate XXIII.2).

(b) Cells large (150–400μm long, 50–150μm broad) bottom
end of frustule rounded. .... **Surirella robusta**
A large and frequent planktonic species. Cells almost
elliptical though narrowing at one end. The narrow end is
rounded rather than pointed, as is the broad end. Costae
1–1.5 per 10μm. Two chromatophores and numerous
pyrenoids. (Plate XXIII.3).

140. (a) Cells sigmoid in outline. **141**
(b) Cells not sigmoid in outline. **144**

141. (a) Cells tapering towards apices. Central raphe and valve
sigmoid **142**

(b) Cells approximately the same width throughout. Cell
apices broadly rounded or truncated. **143**

142. (a) Fine striations transverse and longitudinal. ... **Gyrosigma**
Gyrosigma cells are isopolar and isobilateral. They have
rounded ends. The valve surface has fine striae which are
parallel to the raphe. There are also transverse rows of
punctae. This is a benthic species, mainly epipelic, living
in freshwater, brackish and marine habitats. Two more
common freshwater species are:
G.attenuatum whose cells are 190–250μm long It has
valves with slightly sigmoid ends gradually tapering to
rounded poles. Striations fine, transverse 14–16 in
10μm, longitudinal striations 10–12 in 10μm. Two large
chromatophores present sometimes with jagged edges;
several pyrenoids. Common on various substrata or

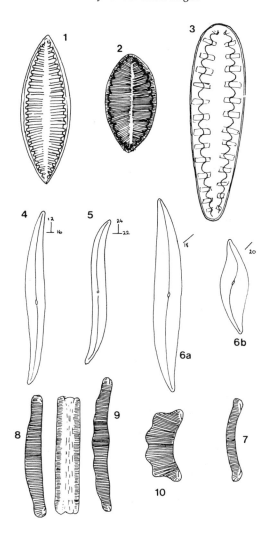

Plate XXIII. 1. **Surirella biserita.** 2. **S.ovalis.** 3. **S.robusta.**
4. **Gyrosigma attenuatum.** 5. **G.spencerii.** 6. **Pleurosigma;**
(a) **P.strigosum,** (b) **P.aestuarii.** 7. **Eunotia exigua.** 8. **E.arcus.**
9. **E.pectinalis.** 10. **E.robusta.**

occasionally in lake or river plankton (Plate XXIII.4 and 5), and **G.spencerii** which has cells only 70–130μm long. **G.spencerii** is smaller than **G.attenuatum** and also has the transverse striae coarser than the longitudinal (17–22 in 10μm as opposed to 22–24 in 10μm). Two large chromatophores present which may have jagged edges; several pyrenoids. Bacillariophyceae.

142. (b)   Valves and raphe sigmoid but striae longitudinal and oblique .... **Pleurosigma**
Cells of **Pleurosigma** are usually solitary, epipelvi and found in marine coastal and brackish waters can extend into salty freshwaters. Valves are sigmoid but not always markedly so. Two or few ribbon-like chloroplasts. A common and widespread genus. Two common species are: **P.strigosum** which has cells 160–300μm in length and is common on muddy shores and in estuaries (and **P.aestuarii** which is smaller having cells 80–150μm in length and is a common coastal species also occurring in the plankton. (Plate XXIII.6).

143. (a)   Girdle and raphe sigmoid, but cells hour-glass shaped in girdle view and naviculoid in valve view ....
.... **Amphiprora** (see 149)

(b)   Frustules somewhat sigmoid in girdle view, central region however with linear sides. Characteristic carinal dots present .... **Nitzschia sigmoidea** (see 152)

144. (a)   Cells distinctly crescent-shaped in outline in valve view ...
.... **145**

(b)   Cells not as above **149**

145. (a)   Frustules crescent-shaped but with outer margin often distinctly undulate. Raphe short only seen on inner margin near apices .... **Eunotia**
Cells of **Eunotia** are arc or crescent shaped often with a distinctly undulate outer edge. Isopolar. Raphe present but shortened and on valve mantle so best seen in girdle view. Striations transverse, punctate. A common benthic species most frequently found in acid waters. **E.exigua** (Plate XXIII.7) does not have an undulate outer margin and is associated with low pH waters (below pH5.6). **E.arcus** is distinctly wider at the centre than towards the ends and has distinctly capitate cells (Plate XXIII.8). **E.pectinalis (XXIII.9)** is very gently arcuate (almost straight) with a gently undulate outer margin (up to 140μm long). **E.robusta** is a shorter broader species (50–90μm long, 17μm wide) with a distinctly undulate outer margin (Plate XXIII.10). The latter three species are all

found in acidic waters for example, with sphagnum. Bacillariophyceae.

145. (b)   Outer margin not undulate, raphe either not visible or an obvious line along apical axis but not short and only near apices of valve margin. **146**

146. (a)   Frustules, although crescent-shaped or arcuate, with one end markedly narrower than the other – heteropolar .... **Rhoicosphenia** Cells of **Rhoicosphenia** have the widest end squared off giving the appearance of a curved wedge. Heterovalvar with the lower valve having a fully developed raphe with central nodules and the upper valve with an extremely reduced raphe in the form of short slits near to the poles. This is not visible using light microscopy only with electron microscopy (Round[7]) so the appearance is one of a pseudoraphe. **Rhoicosphenia curvata** is the only freshwater species which also occurs in the marine environment. Cells 12–75μm long with a single chloroplast. A widely distributed and common epiphyte growing as single cells or more usually stalked fan shaped clusters. (Plate XXIV.1).

(b)   Frustules not as curved wedge **147**

147. (a)   Cells solitary with rounded capitate or rostrate sometimes recurved ends. Typical curved V-shaped marking in central region of valve marking the position of the raphe .... **Epithemia** **Epithemia** is a widely distributed solitary epiphyte sometimes extending into brackish waters but usually favouring base-rich freshwaters. Valves have strongly developed transapical costae with finer punctae between giving a banded appearance. Girdle view rectangular with curved sides. Two of the commoner species are:— **E.turgida** which has broadly rounded recurved poles, a strongly convex outer margin and a less concave inner margin A single large lobed chloroplast is present. Cells 70–200μm in length. **E.zebra** has more lancuolate cells which are gently curved with dorsal and ventral surfaces nearly parallel. Cells 30–150μm long. (Plate XXIV.2 & 3). Bacillariophyceae.

(b)   Cells not as above and without V-shaped raphe. **148**

148. (a)   Valves strongly arched. Asymmetrical frustule 'like a third of an orange' (Hendey[5]). Both raphe systems on ventral surface .... **Amphora** Cells of **Amphora** are normally seen in girdle view and this appears elliptical with truncate ends. The valves are

so arranged that both raphes appear on the relatively flatter ventral face. The dorsal surface strongly arched and is clearly ornamented with transverse punctate striae. Cells solitary, sessile, motile or occasionally free floating. One or more chloroplasts. A very large mainly marine genus but also found in brackish and freshwaters. Some of the more frequent species are indicated below. Bacillariophyceae.

(i)(a) Cells 50–90μm long, rounded apices 10–12 striations in 10μm. Freshwater (Plate XXIV.4). .... **A.ovalis**

(b) Cells less than 50μm long .... **(ii)**

(ii)(a) Cells 30–50μm, weakly capitate apices 20 striations in 10μm. Marine and brackish (Plate XXIV.5). .... **A.coffeaeformis**

(b) Cells not as above .... **(iii)**

(iii)(a) Cells with broadly rounded ends 20 striations in 10μm. Coastal or freshwater (Plate XXIV.6). .... **A.veneta**

(b) Cells with more sharply rounded ends 14–16 striae in 10μm. Freshwater (Plate XXIV.7) .... **A.pediculus**

148. (b) Cells shaped like the segment of an orange but raphe lying either centrally or towards ventral margin – only 1 raphe visible normally. Valve ornamentation more coarse and obvious. .... **Cymbella**

Cells of **Cymbella** may be solitary, colonial or as filaments with individuals enclosed in mucilaginous tubes. Valves crescent or segment shaped but some species are almost lanceolate – isopolar. The raphe position varies from central to very close to the ventral margin. Striae radiate or nearly transverse. Single large lobed chloroplast with central pyrenoid. A large common genus usually attached to surfaces in freshwaters. The more frequent species are indicated below. Bacillariophyceae.

(i)(a) Cells with only slightly curved outside margin nearly lanceolate .... **C.sinuata**

C.sinuata has nearly lanceolate cells with a central raphe. Cells 10–40μm long 4–9μm wide, 911 striae in 10μm. (Plate XXIV.8).

(b) Cells with strongly arcuate or crescent shaped outer margin .... **(ii)**

(ii)(a) Cells small <25μm long .... **C.minuta**

C.minuta is a small species, 10–25μm long with slightly rostrate apices. Striae fine 28–35 in 10μm. Raphe slightly ventral. (Plate XXIV.9).

(b) Cells larger >30μm long .... **(iii)**

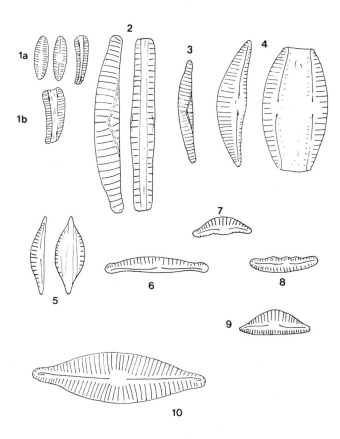

Plate XXIV. 1. Rhoicosphenia. 2. Epithemia turgida. 3. E.zebra. 4. Amphora ovalis. 5. A.coffeaeformis. 6. A.veneta. 7. A.pediculus. 8. Cymbella sinuata 9. C.minuta. 10. C.cuspidata.

(iii)(a)   Cells larger (40)50–160μm .... **(iv)**

  (b)   Cells smaller 30–50(60)μm .... **(vi)**

(iv)(a)   Cells with convex outer and inner margins, capitate ends .... **C.cuspidata**
Cells of **C.cuspidata** are nearly lanceolate with biconvex margins and a central raphe. 40–100μm long, striae 9–10 in 10μm. (Plate XXIV.10).

  (b)   Cells without markedly convex outer and inner margins .. .. **(v)**

(v)(a)   Raphe narrow, central area with 1 to 5 (frequently 3) stigmata .... **C.cistula**
C.cistula cells are 60–160μm long, 18–25μm broad. The clear area around the central nodules of the raphe with frequently 3 stigmata (pores).
(Plate XXV.1)

  (b)   Raphe broad, central area without obvious stigmata .... **C.lanceolata**
C.lanceolata has large cells (up to 210μm). Striae 9–10 in 10μm. (Plate XXV.2).

(vi)(a)   Inner margin slightly convex to nearly straight, outer margin strongly convex .... **C.turgida**
The margins of **C.turgida** are both convex with the outer one markedly so but they do not appear as near lanceolate as in **C.cuspidata**. Cells 35–60μm long. Striae 7–10 in 10μm. (Plate XXV.3).

  (b)   Inner margin straight with slight central bulge, outer margin strongly convex .... **C.gracilis**
C.gracilis has less broadly appearing cells than **C.turgida**. Cells 30–45μm long, 7–10μm broad. Striae 10–13 in 10μm. (Plate XXV.4).

149. (a)   Cells characteristic hour-glass shape in girdle view, lanceolate with sigmoid keel in valve view. . **Amphiprora**
Amphiprora is free living solitary or united in chains or in a flat mucous surround. Valves isopolar. There is a sigmoid raised keel carrying the raphe. Striations fine. Occurs commonly in brackish water or slow moving fresh water, 1–2 chloroplasts. Up to 130μm long. (Plate XXV.5).

  (b)   Cells not hour-glass shaped **150**

150. (a)   Cells with twisted or undulating margin in girdle view. Valves linear or elliptical in valve view sometimes with narrow central region. .... **Cymatopleura**
Cells of **Cymatopleura** are isopolar and isobilateral. Cell apices rounded or pointed. The undulations in the cell wall give a banded lighter and darker appearance in valve

view. Raphe in a wing along the margin. Single large chloroplast. Common bottom living species in freshwaters, especially those rich in dissolved substances. Two of the commoner species are **C.solea** in which the cells are elongate (30–150μm long) with valve margins almost parallel and only a small central constriction and **C.elliptica** which is broadly elliptical with no central constriction (cells 80–200μm long). (Plate XXV.6 7). Bacillariophyceae.

150. (b) Cells not twisted or undulating in girdle view. **151**
151. (a) Each valve bearing carinal dots. No visible (clear central area **152**
   (b) No carinal dots present **153**
152. (a) Keel of each valve visible on same girdle face. ....
.... **Hantzschia**
Cells are unattached and benthic, freshwater or marine. The commonest freshwater species is **Hantzschia amphioxys**, occurring either in the plankton or often in abundance on damp soil. Cells 20–100μm long. 5–10μm broad. Valves slightly convex on one face, slightly concave on the other, rostrate. Transverse striations present 13–20 in 10μm. Carinal dots 5–8 in 10μm. Usually two, plate-like, chromatophores.
(Plate XXV.8).

   (b) Keel of each valve diagonally opposite. .... **Nitzschia**
Cells of **Nitzschia** are elliptical, linear or sigmoid in valve view. The raphe is displaced to one margin but the raphes of each valve are diagonally opposite. The raphe structure itself is supported by bars which appear as the carinal dots under light microscopy. There is no clear central area and the valve is decorated with transverse striae of punctae which can be fine or coarse. Two large chloroplasts are present. Cells are solitary and may be benthic or planktonic, marine, brackish or freshwater. Very many species – common. The more frequently occurring species are described below. Bacillariophyceae.

   (i)(a) Valves spindle-shaped with drawn out needle-like extremities .... **N.acicularis**
Cells of **N.acicularis** are between 50–150μm long and 3–4μm broad. They are spindle-shaped with elongated poles. The walls are not heavily silicified; and wall markings, except for the carinal dots, are hardly visible. Carinal dots 17–20 in 10μm. This fairly small and delicate species is capable of quite rapid movements. It is widely distributed and often abundant in lakes, ponds etc. (Plate XXV.9).

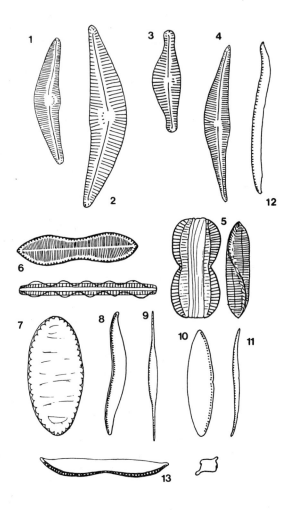

Plate XXV. 1. Cymbella cistula. 2. C.lanceolata. 3. C.turgida. 4. C.gracilis. 5. Amphiprora. 6. Cymatopleura solea. 7. C.elliptica. 8. Hantzschia amphioxys. 9. Nitzschia acicularis. 10. N.tryblionella. 11. N.sigma. 12. N.sigmoidea. 13 N.bilobata

(i)(b)   Valves not spindle-shaped with needle-like extremities ....
.... **(ii)**

(ii)(a)   Valves elliptical, only 3 to 5 times as long as broad ....
.... **N.tryblionella**
Valves of **N.tryblionella** are much broader and more
elliptical than in most other species. Cells 70–80μm long
20–30μm broad. The valve striations are very fine (30–35
in 10μm). Common in estuaries, harbours and muddy
brackish areas and in freshwater. (Plate XXV.10).

(b)   Valves other shape .... **(iii)**

(iii)(a)   Cells sigmoid in valve view .... **(iv)**

(b)   Cells not sigmoid in valve view .... **(v)**

(iv)(a)   Valves with narrow attenuated rostrate apices. . **N.sigma**
Cells of **N.sigma** are 90–250μm long and 12–15μm wide.
They are lanceolate gradually tapering towards the ends.
Striae 2–24 in 10μm, 7–9 carinal dots in 10μm. Common
in freshwater, brackish and marine habitats. (Plate
XXV.11).

(b)   Valves almost linear are parallel at the centre only curving
at the end to give apiculate apices. .... **N.sigmoidea**
N.sigmoidea cells are 90–500μm long and 8–14μm broad.
Striae 23–26 in 10μm and carinal dots 5–7 in 10μm. A
common benthic freshwater species. (Plate XXV.12).

(v)(a)   Valves distinctly bilobate .... **N.bilobata**
Valves of **N.bilobata** are linear to lanceolate with apiculate
to rostrate apices and with a marked constriction in the
centre. Cells 80–130μm long, 15–18μm wide. Striae 16–19
in 10μm, carinal dots 5–7 in 10μm. Common benthic form
in coastal waters, brackish waters and freshwaters. (Plate
XXV.13)

(b)   Valves not distinctly bilobed .... **(vi)**

(vi)(a)   Cells long > 65μm .... **(vii)**

(b)   Cells smaller < 60μm .... **(viii)**

(vii)(a)   Cells large, 70–180μm long, 5–6μm wide, linear lanceolate
in shape, small constriction in middle of valve along
raphe edge .... **N.linearis**
N.linearis is a freshwater common species, especially in
shallow waters. The valves have a small medium
constriction but otherwise generally straight-sided and
have small capitate poles. Transverse striations 28–30 in
10μm, carinal dots 7–10 in 10μm. (Plate XXVI.1).

(b)   Cells 60–100μm long, 8–9μm wide, weakly concave sides
and broader than **N.linearis**. Apices capitate ....
.... **N.hungarica**
A very widely distributed species in salt and brackish

waters and extending into freshwaters 16–18 striae in 10μm, 9–10 carinal dots in 10μm. (Plate XXVI.2).

(viii)(a)   Striae heavy 16–20 in 10μm with coarse punctae. ..... **(ix)**

(b)   Striae fine 30–36 in 10μm with very fine punctae ...... **(xi)**

(ix)(a)   Valve lanceolate, apices rostrate carinal dots 8–9 in 10μm, striae 16 in 10μm. Cells 20–35μm long, 4–5μm wide .... **N.amphibia**
N.amphibia is a common freshwater benthic species. (Plate XXVI.3).

(b)   Valve linear tapering to sub-acute apices 8–10 carinal dots in 10μm, striae 20–22 in 10μm. Cells 20–40μm long, 5μm wide .... **N.frustulum**
N.frustulum is a common freshwater, brackish water and estuarine species. (Plate XXVI.4).

(x)(a)   Valve linear to lanceolate with slightly rostrate apices. Carinal dots 10–12 in 10μm striae 33–36 in 10μm .... **N.palea**
N.palea is a very common freshwater species. Cells 20–60μm long, 4–5μm wide, tends to be more common in enriched/polluted waters. (Plate XXVI.5).

(b)   Valves more broadly rounded, carinal dots 10–11 in 10μm, striae 30 in 10μm .... **N.communis**
A common freshwater species, mainly benthic. (Plate XXVI.6).

153. (a)   Cells heteropolar with one end much larger than the other **154**

(b)   Cells isopolar or only just heteropolar **157**

154. (a)   Cells with longitudinal axis; curved or crescent-shaped ... . **Rhoicosphenia** (see 146)

(b)   Cells with longitudinal axis straight **155**

155. (a)   Cells cunate in valve and girdle views. Rim of valve face with short thick spines which may be difficult to see .... **Peronia**
Cells of **Peronia** are solitary and attached by means of a mucilaginous stalk. A short raphe is present on one valve with a rudimentary one or other valve. Very narrow axial area, striae fine. Frequent in acid oligotrophic waters especially with sphagnum. (Plate XXVI.7). Bacillariophyceae.

(b)   Cells club shaped, clavate often with an inflated centre section. Ends variable capitate to apiculate **156**

156. (a)   Cells large, 100–150μm long, wide at centre then narrowing towards ends which are enlarged and rounded. The apical one being larger than the other. Distinct unornamental area at apex of smaller end .... **Didymosphenia**

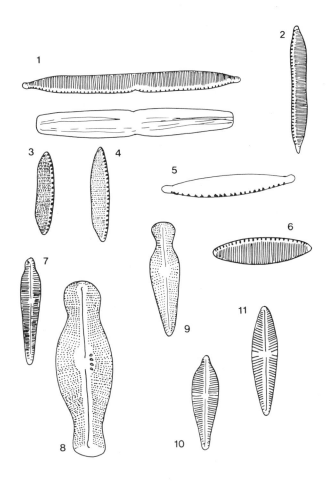

Plate XXVI. 1. Nitzschia linearis. 2. N.hungarica. 3. N.amphibia.
4. N.frustulum. 5. N.palea. 6. N.communis. 7. Peronia.
8. Didymosphenia. 9. Gomphonema constrictum. 10. G.parvulum.
11. G.olivaceum

Cells heteropolar, with capitate ends. Raphe central and straight. Transverse striae of coarse punctae radiant around central clear area Striae 8–10 on 10µm. Central clear area rounded with 2–4 stigmata. Cells isolated epiphytic or epilithic attached by means of mucilaginous stalks. Found in alkaline waters where it may occur in large numbers. (Plate XXVI.8). Bacillariophyceae.

158. (b)   Cells smaller, < 100µm, although often wider at centre, usually tapering towards rear pole which is often acute and towards the front which is more variable in shape – rounded, apiculate or capitate. Striae of finer punctae. ...

.... **Gomphomema**

Cells of **Gomphomema** are somewhat club shaped or like a small **Didymosphenia** (Egyptian mummy shape) and wedge shaped in girdle view. They are very common epiphytes attached by mucilaginous stalks. Occurs in a wide range of waters including those enriched with sewage. Three common species are **G.constrictum** which has cells 25–65µm long with a broad flattened apical pole with a constriction behind it, **G.parvulum** which is club shaped, 12–30µm long and has 14–16 striae in 20µm. It also has a single stigmata in the clear central area. **G.olivaceum** is a similar shape, 15–40µm long, 11–14 striae in 10µm but has a clear central area with no stigmata. All have a single lobed chloroplast with one central pyrenoid. (Plate XXVI.9 to 11).

157. (a)   Valves bent (genuflexed) in girdle view, linear to elliptical

.... **Achnanthes**

Cells of **Achnanthes** are heterovalvar, one valve bearing a true raphe, the other a pseudoraphe. Shape of ends variable. Raphe and pseudoraphe usually central but can be diagonal but may be displaced towards one edge. Striations transverse, may differ on each valve. Some species have a horse-shoe shaped mark at the edge centre of the raphless valve. Two to many chloroplasts per cell. This is a very common benthic group, mostly marine but freshwater as well. Five of the common species are indicated below. Bacillariophyceae.

(i)(a)   Cells large, usually greater than 50µm, with obvious median constriction .... **A.longipes**

Cells of **A.longipes** are elongate, tapering towards the pole, with acute apices and with a noticeable median constriction. Valve surface coarsely punctate. Pseudoraphe slightly eccentric, raphe enclosed in stout rib and at centre area transverses the cell to produce a cross or stauros shape. Many chloroplasts per cell. Cells (40) 50–160μm long 12–28μm broad. A very common sessile littoral species in shallow coastal waters. Cells united into filaments of up to 60 cells attached by a mucous stalk. (Plate XXVII.1).

(i)(b)   Cells smaller < 40μm without median constriction. .... **ii**

(ii)(a)   Cells with horse-shoe shaped markings, on valve with pseudoraphe, near centre margin. .... **A.lanceolata**
Cells lanceolate to elliptical with gently convex margins. Poles rounded, slightly truncated. Pseudoraphe and raphe central to their respective valves. Horse-shoe shaped marking to one side of the pseudoraphe valve. Cells 17–35μm long, 5–8μm broad 12–13 striae in 10μm. Found in nutrient rich waters. (Plate XXVII.2).

(b)   Cells without horse-shoe shaped marking on pseudoraphe valve .... **(iii)**

(iii)(a)   Cells with swollen mid-region narrowing to capitate/ sub-capitate ends .... **A.exigua**
Cells of **A.exigua** are lanceolate to elliptical, swollen around the centre but with narrower capitate ends. Raphe valve with transverse clear area at centre. Cells 15–30μm long. (Plate XXVII.3).

(b)   Cells not broadly swollen in mid-region, margins slightly convex .... **(iv)**

(iv)(a)   Frustules gradually tapering towards the poles. ....
.... **A.minutissima**
Cells of **A.minutissima** are linear-elliptic, narrowing to rounded poles. Cells 2–4μm broad, 15–20μm long, transverse striae 33–35 in 10μm. Raphe delicate and thread-like, pseudoraphe narrow without central clear area. Abundant as an epiphyte and on stones, etc., especially in flowing waters. Tolerant of metal pollution. (Plate XXVII.4).

(b)   Frustules constricted towards capitate poles. ....
.... **A.microcephala**
A.microcephala is abundant as a stalked epiphyte especially on other algae. Cells 2–3μm broad, 18–26μm long, linear-lanceolate in shape with a constriction below the rounded, capitate, poles. Raphe slender, as is pseudoraphe. Central area hardly in evidence. Tolerant of metal pollution. (Plate XXVII.5).

157. (b)   Cells not crooked or bent in girdle view **158**

158. (a)   Valves lanceolate to elliptical, striae finely punctate transverse to slightly medial interrupted by a broad transverse clear area (stauros) extending from margin to

A Key to Common Algae

margin. .... **Stauroneis**
Stauroneis is a widespread benthic freshwater and marine littoral species. Cell ends may be rounded rostrate capitate or slightly pointed. Some species have a pseudoseptum at the ends giving the cell apex a halo appearance. Raphe area narrow. Two frequent species are **S.acuta** which has rhomboid to lanceolate cells, slightly rounded poles and central region and polar septa (cells 80–166μm long) and **S.phoenicentron** which are lanceolate with convex margins. There is no swollen central area and no polar septa. (Cells 70–325μm long). (Plate XXVII.6).

158. (b)   Valves without stauros **159**
159. (a)   Cells linear to lanceolate. Clear narrow centre axial area joining the two portions of the raphe which are shortened and situated within a thickened rib towards the poles and extends about 1/3 the way into the centre .. **Amphipleura**
Valves of **Amphipleura** are isopolar with rounded ends. The raphe arrangement is characteristic. The valve surface is covered with extremely fine parallel striae. Cells 80–140μm long, 7–10μm broad. **A.pellucida** is the commonest freshwater species and **A.rutilans** the commonest marine coastal species. The cells are solitary or in mucilaginous colonies. (Plate XXVII.7 & 8). Bacillariophyceae.

159. (b)   Cells not as above **160**
160. (a)   Cells linear or linear lanceolate. Central axis usually with narrow clear area – a pseudoraphe. Striae parallel ....
.... **Synedra**
Cells of **Synedra** may either be solitary or bunched irregularly or in stellate colonies. They may be attached or free. The parallel striae may be absent from the central region in some species. Two large chloroplasts sometimes disintegrating into a number of smaller plates, 3 or more pyrenoids. **Synedra** is a common widely distributed genus in both fresh and salt water. Three of the more common freshwater species are described below. Bacillariophyceae.

(i)(a)   Cells linear with capitate ends and no clear central area ..
.... **S.capitata**
Cells of **S.capitata** have distinctly capitate ends, 125–500μm long 10μm broad. Striae 7–8 in 10μm. A common epiphyte. (Plate XXVII.9).

(b)   Cells without distinctly capitate ends .... **(ii)**
(ii)(a)   Cells linear, apices rostrate or sharply tapering .... **S.ulna**
A common, sometimes abundant, and widely distributed

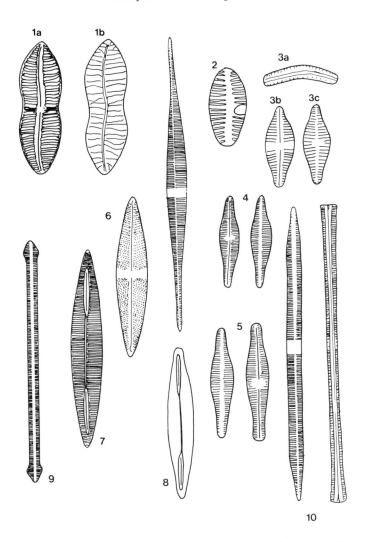

Plate XXVII. 1. Achnanthes longipes. 2. A.lanceolata. 3. A.exigua. 4. A.minutissima. 5. A.microcephala. 6. Stauroneis phoenicentron. 7. Amphipleura pellucida. 8. A.rutilans. 9. Synedra capitata. 10. S.ulna. 11. S.acus

species. Cells 70–400μm long 5–9μm broad. There is usually a clear central area. Striae 8–12 in 10μm. (Plate XXVII.10).

(ii)(b)   Cells fusiform – gradually tapering towards the rounded or slightly capitate apices. .... **S.acus**
Cells are needle-like or fusiform, 5–6μm broad at centre, 1.5μm broad at apex. Length 100–300μm. Striae 12–14 in 10μm. Small clear central area. Common and widely distributed. (Plate XXVII.11).

NB. Synedra can be difficult to distinguish from Fragilaria in cleaned material.

160. (b)   Cells elongate, sometimes boat shaped, with rounded or more or less pointed ends, true raphe present as are central and polar nodules **161**

161. (a)   Valves with coarse transverse to slightly radial striae (alveoli) not composed of punctae. .... **Pinnularia**
Cells of **Pinnularia** are solitary linear to elongate elliptical. Poles usually broadly rounded. Raphe central and may be fine or broad. Centrally the raphe ends usually turn to the same side. Two plate like chloroplasts. A very common benthic species, mainly freshwater, often abundant especially in poorer waters. Two more frequent species are **P.viridis** which has elongate to elliptical cells, 50–170μm long, 10–30μm broad with transverse striae very close to each other (almost touching (6–9 in 10μm), and **P.alpina** whose cells are elliptical to lanceolate, 100–280μm long and 328–58μm broad. The transverse striae are very coarse and distinctly separated from one another (2–4 in 10μm). (Plate XXVIII.1&2).

(b)   Valves with finer striae or punctate **162**

162. (a)   Valves lanceolate or rhomboidal, isopolar. Raphe contained within two parallel ribs running from central area to near the apices .... **Frustulia**
The frequently rhomboidal valves of **Frustulia** have rounded edges and poles. They are symmetrical. The raphe itself is thread like and straight. It is enclosed within two ribs (which are actually internal) which fuse at the poles and central region. The valve surface with fine parallel striations. Occurs as single cells or occasionally as mucous filaments. Predominantly freshwater but also occurring in brackish habitats. Two of the more common species are:— **F.vulgaris** with striations somewhat more radially arranged around the central area. Cells 40–80μm long, 10–13 broad. Striae 14 in 10μm near centre 34 in

10μm near the poles. One two lobed chloroplasts. Cells often enclosed in a mucilage tube. Common, especially on damp soils (Plate XXVIII.3). **F.rhomboides** has striations which are all transverse. The frustule is distinctly rhomboidal in shape. Cells are often enclosed in mucilage and are common in acid streams and bogs. Cells 70–160μm long 15–30μm broad. Striae 23–30 in 10μm. (Plate XXVIII.4). Bacillariophyceae.

162. (b) Raphe not contained within parallel ribs **163**

163. (a) Transverse striae consisting of punctae which may be very fine **164**

(b) Transverse striae consists of fine or slightly coarser lines (alveolate) **166**

164. (a) Striae fine transverse (or slightly angled towards poles), crossed near valve margin and parallel to it by a longitudinal line (ore more than 1 line). Raphe forked at poles although sometimes difficult to see .... **Neidium**
Cells of **Neidium** are lanceolate to elliptical, isopolar. Poles rounded, capitate or rostrate. Narrow axial area, central area roundish. Striae punctate but characteristically interrupted by the parallel lines near the margin. 4 chloroplasts – usually one in each quarter of the cell. A common but not abundant, widely distributed solitary freshwater genus. **N.iridis** which has large (90–200μm long 20–30μm broad) cells linear to lanceolate in shape. Striae 22–29 in 10μm. The raphe is straight with ends pointing in opposite directions at the centre. **N.affine** has distinctly capitate ends and is smaller (cells 30–90μm long, 6–10μm broad). Striae 22–30 in 10μm. Raphe as in **N.iridis**. Finally **N.dubium** is a shorter (30–40μm long) broader (10μm wide) species with more sharply rostrate ends. (Plate XXVIII. 5 to 7).

(b) Striae not crossed by lines parallel end near to the valve margin **165**

165. (a) Valve with striations composed of punctae arranged in irregular lines – gives a dashed appearance. Central area round or angular. .... **Anomoeoneis**
Cells of **Anomoeoneis** are solitary benthic mostly freshwater but occasionally brackish. Valves lanceolate to elliptical, isopolar. Raphe central, fine. Single chloroplast. **Anomoeoneis** and **Brachysira** were originally combined. **Anomoeoneis** occurs in high conductivity water. **Brachysira** is common in oligotrophic acidic waters. The latter also has the raphe enclosed within small but noticeable parallel ribs.

A.exilis is a frequent species. Cells 15–35μm long, 4–6μm broad, lanceolate with sub-capitate poles. **A.sphaerophora** is larger (40–80μm long, 13–20μm broad) with the cells elliptical to lanceolate with rostrate ends. (Plate XXVIII.8&9). Bacillariophyceae.

165. (b) Valve striations regular without dashed appearance ....

.... **Navicula** (in part see 166)
The genus **Navicula** is extremely large and diverse. Often species which could not be placed elsewhere were placed here. Perhaps true **Navicula** species are those with alveoli (see section) which are in the section **Lineolatae** of the genus. Two common punctate species are **N.cuspidata** which has lanceolate valves 30–120μm long, with striae composed of punctae forming both transverse and longitudinal lines, and **N.placenta** is also lanceolate but smaller (35–45μm long) and the punctae form obvious transverse striae but not vertical lines. (Plate XXVIII.10&11).

166. (a) Valves with more punctate (alveolate) striae and with one or more longitudinal lines running parallel to the margin .

.... **Caloneis**
Caloneis cells are lanceolate to elliptical, isopolar. The poles may be rounded or capitate. Central area round or angular sometimes extending to valve margin. Striae fine transverse but crossed by one or two longitudinal lines close to and parallel to the margin. Cells are unattached freshwater or marine. Two common shaped capitate ends and a distinctly swollen central region (cells 25–120μm long, 10–20μm broad) and **C.amphisbaena** which has broadly elliptical cells with capitate ends. Cells 30–80μm long, 20–30μm broad. Very closely related to **Pinnularia**. Common, often in richer waters. (Plate XXIX.1).

166. (b) Valves with alveolae but without longitudinal lines parallel to the margin. .... **Navicula** (in part see 165).
Navicula is a large and diverse genus which is often divided into a number of sections. With more intensive investigations using electron microscopy the group is undergoing continuous revision. For detailed identification of the numerous species more specialised texts are required (see Bibliography).
Cells of **Navicula** are solitary boat shaped (naviculoid). Two chloroplasts are present each with a pyrenoid. Valves lanceolate or linear with a flat or gently curved surface. Striae usually radiate around clear central area, but may be transverse towards the end. Raphe straight fine and

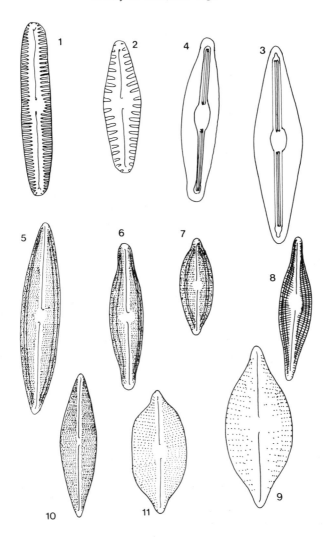

Plate XXVIII. 1. Pinnularia viridis. 2. P.alpina. 3. Frustulia vulgaris. 4. F.rhomboides. 5. Neidium iridis. 6. N.affine. 7. N.dubium. 8. Anomoeoneis exilis. 9. A.sphaerophora. 10. Navicula cuspidata. 11. N.placenta.

central. Freshwater or marine very common indeed. A selection of some more common species are indicated below.

(i)(a)   Cells small, 4–8μm long, elliptical .... **N.atomus**
N.atomus is a small elliptical species with fine markings (30 striae in 10μm). Common freshwater epilithic species. (Plate XXIX.2).

(b)   Cells larger > 20μm .... **(ii)**

(ii)(a)   Striations, very fine, 40–45 in 10μm, valves linear with capitate ends .... **N.subtilissima**
N.subtilissima cells are 30–35μm long 5–8μm broad. Freshwater, in rivers. (Plate XXIX.3).

(b)   Striations more coarse 20 in 10μm .... **(iii)**

(iii)(a)   Valves rhomboid to lanceolate .... **N.rhombica**
Valves are weakly rhomboid. Central area elliptical. Cells 60–90μm long 16–20 wide. Striae 10–20 in 10μm. A common marine species. (Plate XXIX.4).

(b)   Valves not rhomboidal .... **(iv)**

(iv)(a)   Valves elliptical to lanceolate .... **(v)**

(b)   Valves lanceolate .... **(vi)**

(v)(a)   Cells larger, 30–60μm long, 6–12μm broad, striae mediate at centre, large rounded central area, 12 striae in 10μm ..
.... **N.lanceolata**
A common freshwater and marine species. (Plate XXIX.5).

(b)   Cells elliptical to lanceolate 25–35μm long 5–7 broad. 16–18 striae in 10μm .... **N.cryptocephala**
A common freshwater and marine form.
(Plate XXIX.6).

(vi)(a)   Valves lanceolate with extended subacute apices. Cells 36–44μm long. Striae 13–14 in 10μm. .... **N.phyllepta**
A common brackish water and freshwater species. (Plate XXIX.7).

(b)   Valves without extended apices .... **(vii)**

(vii)(a)   Valve striae radiate around central area .... **(viii)**

(b)   Valve striae transverse throughout. .... **N.ramosissima**
This is a colonial form living in branching mucous tubes. Cells 34–42μm long, 5μm broad. Striae 12 in 10μm. Marine growing on hard surfaces. (Plate XXIX.8).

(viii)(a)   Cells large 30–60μm. Striae 11–12 in 10μm with rectangular clear central area. Rounded ends. Lanceolate to linear ..
.... **N.tripunctata**
A very common freshwater species. (Plate XXIX.9).

(b)   Cells smaller 24–36μm long. Striae 12–13 in 10μm strongly radiate in central region which is slightly irregular. The central striae are more pronounced than the apical ones .

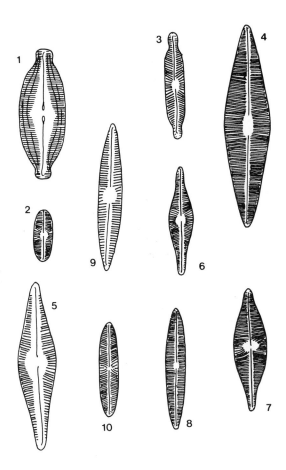

Plate XXIX. 1. Caloneis amphisbaena. 2. Navicula atomus. 3. N.subtilissima. 4. N.rhombica. 5. N.lanceolata. 6. N.cryptocephala. 7. N.phyllepta. 8. N.ramosissima. 9. N.tripunctata. 10. N.cincta

.... **N.cincta**
A common freshwater and marine species.
(Plate XXIX.10).

167. (a)   Cells ovoid to spherical **168**
NB. See Glossary for definitions of shapes.

(b)   Cells other shape (cells with median groove, although possibly ovoid in general outline, are included here) **173**

168. (a)   Cells bearing spines **169**

(b)   Cells without spines **172**

169. (a)   Cells spherical or only very slightly oval **170**

(b)   Cells oval to elliptical **171**

170. (a)   Cells solitary, spherical, 7–15μm in diameter, numerous fairly long spines. .... **Golenkinia radiata**
Golenkinia radiata cells are solitary, but occasionally form false colonies by failing to separate immediately after division. There are several spines per cell (12 or more) 24–45μm long. Single cup-shaped chloroplast with a pyrenoid. Planktonic. (Plate XXX.1). Chlorophyceae.

(b)   Cells solitary, though usually in colonies of 48–16, ovoid to spherical, 3–7μm diameter. 1–5 spines 20–35μm long ..
.... **Micractinium** (see 92)

171. (a)   Cells with two spines arising at each pole. ....
.... **Lagerheimia quadriseta**
Lagerheimia quadriseta has ovate cells 4–6–6.5μm in diameter, 7.5–12μm long. The two spines at each pole are up to 23μm long. There are 1–4 chloroplasts and pyrenoids may be present. Planktonic in lakes or ponds. (Plate XXX.2). Chlorophyceae.

(b)   Cells with 3–8 spines arising from each pole. . **Chodatella**
Cells oblong to ovate, 6–18μm in diameter, 10–21μm long. 1–4 chromatophores with a pyrenoid. Spines fine 15–20μm long. Planktonic in lakes and ponds. (Plate XXX.3). Chlorophyceae.

172. (a)   Cells small < 10μm, roughly spherical in shape. ....
.... **Chlorella**
Cells of **Chlorella** are spherical to sub-spherical with a single parietal chloroplast which nearly fills the cell and a single pyrenoid. Cells common in eutrophic waters but their small size makes them easily overlooked. Two of the more frequent species are **C.pyrenoidosa** which has small cells 3–5μm broad and **C.vulgaris** which has larger cells, 5–10μm broad. (Plate XXX.4&5).

(b)   Cells ovoid, larger > 10μm in size .... **Oocystis**
Cells of **Oocystis** are ovoid to egg-shaped either solitary or in colonies of 2–4–8–16 enclosed by the mother cell

wall. Chloroplasts disc-shaped or plate-like. A common widespread species in lakes and ponds, some species in softer waters others in enriched harder waters. The commoner species are indicated below. Chlorophyceae.

(i)(a) Cells ovoid with polar thickenings .... **(ii)**

(b) Cells without polar thickenings .... **(iii)**

(ii)(a) Chloroplasts 4–10, cells 10–20μm broad, 14–26μm long ...
.... **Oocystis crassa**
Common in the plankton. Solitary or in groups of 1–8 enclosed within the old mother cell wall. Pyrenoids usually present. (Plate XXX.6).

(b) Chloroplasts 12–25, cells 3–9μm broad, 7–20μm long ......
.... **Oocystis solitaria**
Cells usually solitary. Pyrenoids present. Very common in the plankton. Polar nodules conspicuous. (Plate XXX.7).

(iii)(a) Cells ovoid to fusiform with pointed ends. 1–3 disc shaped chloroplasts per cell .... **O.parva**
O.parva is either solitary or occurs in groups of 2–8 cells within the mother cell wall. Cells 6–16μm long 4–8μm in diameter. (Plate XXX.8).

(b) Cells not fusiform, chloroplasts more than 3 per cell **(iv)**

(iv)(a) Cells large, 40–50μm long .... **O.gigas**
Cells of **Oocystis gigas** are large and are usually grouped in 4s within a smooth mother cell wall. Many disc shaped chloroplasts. (Plate XXX.9).

(b) Cells smaller < 40μm long .... **(v)**

(v)(a) Cells 20–30μm long, 4–8 stellate plate like chloroplasts ...
.... **O.natans**
Cells of **O.natans** are ellipsoidal with no polar thickenings. (Plate XXX.10).

(b) Cells 15–25μm long, ellipsoidal. Usually 2–4–8 cells within irregular mother cell wall. Numerous (10+) disc shaped chloroplasts .... **O.elliptica**
Common in the plankton (Plate XXX.11).

173. (a) Cells having a distinct median groove **174**

(b) Cells without a median groove **180**

174. (a) Cells five-sided, angles rounded and tipped with a short spine. One side with a deep groove. ....
.... **Tetraedron caudatum**
Cells 8–22μm in diameter, pentagonal but with rounded angles each bearing a single short spine. Chromatophores 1 to many, usually with pyrenoids. Common but rarely abundant in lowland waters.
(Plate XXX.12). Chlorophyceae.

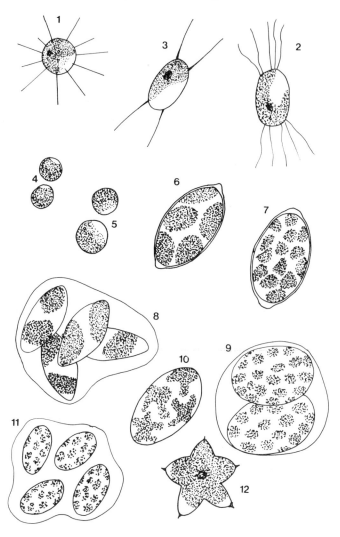

Plate XXX. 1. Golenkenia radiata. 2. Lagerheimia quadriseta. 3. Chodatella. 4. Chlorella pyrenoidosa. 5. C.vulgaris. 6. Oocystis crass. 7. O.solitaria. 8. O.parva. 9. O.gigas. 10. O.natans. 11. O.elliptica. 12. Tetraedron caudatum.

174. (b)   Cells not as above, the groove being equal on two sides **175**

175. (a)   Overall shape of cells cylindrical to sub-cylindrical ... **176**

(b)   Cells not cylindrical in shape **178**

176. (a)   Cells a straight, elongate cylinder (X10 lab). Noticeable constriction in centre not deep. .... **Pleurotaenium** The median constriction is not deep and there may be a swelling either side of it. Often a thickening around central area of constriction. Cells 20–650μm in length. Chloroplasts numerous longitudinal bands with pyrenoids. Often in soft more acid waters. (Plate XXXI.1). Chlorophyceae.

(b)   Cells not a straight elongate cylinder but a shorter more rounded cylinder **177**

177. (a)   Cells cylindrical to fusiform, large 150–240μm long .... **Tetmemorus** Cells are rounded cylinders with an open median constriction. Characteristic deep narrow incision in cell apices. Chloroplast – one in each semicell with numerous pyrenoids. Cell wall may be granulate. Common in ponds and acid pools. (Plate XXXI.2). Chlorophyceae.

(b)   Cells short cylinders (sub-cylindrical) and more rounded, smaller 60–80μm long .... **Actinotaenium** Cells of **Actinotaenium** are only short being a little like an elongate **Cosmarium** but with only a shallow medium constriction. Wall with very fine punctae. Stellate chloroplast with pyrenoid. Common amongst other algae in ponds. (Plate XXXI.3). Chlorophyceae.

178. (a)   Median groove wide, cells with horns or, if not, of polygonal shape .... **Staurastrum** **Staurastrum** is an extremely large genus of desmids. The cells are divided into two semicells with a wide median groove or isthmus. The angles of the semicells are produced into horns or processes which may sometimes be short or stumpy giving the cell a polygonal appearance. In apical view the cells are usually triangular but may have ten processes. The cell wall may be smooth or have ornamentation. **Staurastrum** is probably the most frequent desmid in the plankton. Some species secrete a mucilaginous surround. They occur in all freshwaters ranging from oligotrophic to eutrophic but are more frequent in upland areas. Some of the more common species are indicated below but more detailed texts might need to be consulted.

(i)(a)   Angles of semicells without developed processes or horns – overall appearance triangular or polygonal .... **(ii)**

(b)   Angles of semicells with well defined processes or horns – usually three per semicell (triradiate) but may be more ... **(v)**

(ii)(a)   Cells without spines, cell wall smooth or finely punctate .. .. **(iii)**

(b)   Cells with spines or granulate wall .... **(iv)**

(iii)(a)   Semicells elliptical with rounded edges 20–43μm long. (Plate XXXI.4) .... **S.muticum**

(b)   Semicells with flatter sides and apices fine punctae over surface. 20–60μm long.(Plate XXXI.5) .... **S.orbiculare**

(iv)(a)   Cell wall markedly granulate with a pattern of concentric rings from each cell apex. Cells with mucilaginous surround. (Plate XXXI.6). .... **S.punctulatum**

(b)   Cells with one or more spines at the angles. Semicells triangular with rounded sides. Cell wall punctate 70–120μm long, spines 10–30μm long. (Plate XXXI.7) .... **S.longispinum**

(v)(a)   Median groove relatively narrow acutely angled. Processes and body, with short pointed punctae or spines. Processes length just over width of body .... **S.anatinum** **S.anatinum** is a common species with many varieties. (Plate XXXI.8).

(b)   Median groove wide with obtuse angle. Processes slender and much longer than width of body. .... **(vi)**

(vi)(a)   Processes or horns × 2 lengths of body. Short spines on outer surface of semicell (ie not around isthmus region). Processes slender. .... **S.planctonicum** A common species in the plankton of lakes. The processes of each semicell may be parallel although they can be divergent. Processes with 3 spines at end). Cells 45–80μm long including processes. (Plate XXXI.9).

(b)   Processes 1½–2 × length of body. Isthmus with ring of short spines either side. .... **S.cingulum** The wall is covered with more spines than in **S.planctonicum** with a marked ring either side of the isthmus. Processes terminate in 3 spines. Cells 30–70μm long. (Plate XXXI.10).

178. (b)   Median groove narrow, or if wider cells with smooth wall and single spine at apex **179**

179. (a)   Median groove marked – acute to obtuse. Semicells, roughly triangular, each apex with one spine .... **Staurodesmus** **Staurodesmus** is a genus combining **Arthrodesmus** and the smooth bodied **Staurodiscmus** without processes but with single spines. A very common genus in the plankton or in amongst macrophytes.

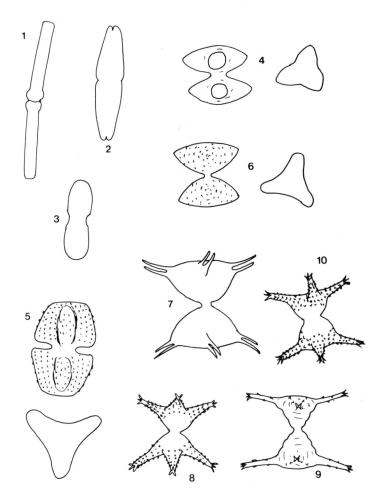

Plate XXXI. 1. Pleurotaenium. 2. Tetmemorus. 3. Actinotaenium. 4. Staurastrum muticum. 5. S.orbiculare. 6. S.punctulatum. 7. S.longispinum. 8. S.anatinum. 9. S.planctonicum. 10. S.cingulum

S.subulatus has an acute isthmus, it is biradiate with parallel long spines. (Plate XXXII.1).

S.jaculiferous is triradiate with an obtuse isthmus and divergent spines. (Plate XXXII.2). For more detailed identification the reader should consult one of the specialist texts listed in the Bibliography. Chlorophyceae.

179. (b) Median groove very narrow, overall shape of cell ovoid to rounded (although angles may be flattened). Semicells not extended into processes. No spines present. Cell outline entire, no indentations .... **Cosmarium**

Cosmarium cells are rounded with a narrow (usually) or slightly wider median groove. The walls are usually covered with granulations, spines are absent. Granulations may be fine and not easily seen. Very widespread and common. The largest desmid genus occurs in a wide range of waters. Only four of the more common species are indicated below and readers are advised to consult the more specialised texts for detailed identification. Chlorophyceae.

(i)(a) Cell wall smooth .... **Cosmarium bioculatum**
Cells small, 15–20μm long, 15–21μm wide. Semicells oblong to elliptical without markings on walls. Very widely distributed.
(Plate XXXII.3).

(b) Cell wall with punctae .... **(ii)**

(ii)(a) Cells 1½ times as long as broad, semicells truncated pyramids, punctae small. Cells 58–100μm long ....
.... **Cosmarium pyramidatum**
Generally distributed in peaty waters especially in the north of the British Isles. Cells 58–100μm long, 45–62μm broad. (Plate XXXII.4)

(b) Cells not more than 1½ times as long as broad, semicells oval to reniform, smaller than 55μm long .... **(iii)**

(iii)(a) Cells nearly as long as broad, semicells roughly oval with coarse granulations. .... **Cosmarium praemorsum**
Widely distributed especially in shallow waters. Cells 47–55μm long, 43–51μ broad. (Plate XXXII.5).

(b) Cells not more than 1½ times as long as broad, semicells reniform with fine granulations. **Cosmarium rectangulare**
Widely distributed throughout Britain. Cells 37–47μm long, 30–36μm broad. (Plate XXXII.6).

180. (a) Cells usually in groups of 2–4–8 or more, united along part (in some species the whole) of the lateral walls, spines sometimes present. .... **Scenedesmus** (see 97)

(b) Cells not usually united as above **181**

181. (a)   Cells tetragonal/polygonal, may have spines at angles .... **Tetraedron**
Tetraedron has angular cells with or without spines. Single chloroplast with one to many pyrenoids. Common but not abundant in the freshwater plankton. Three common species are listed below. Chlorophyceae.

   (i)(a)   Cell angles with short spines .... **(ii)**

    (b)   Cell angles without short spines .... **(iii)**

  (ii)(a)   Cells tetragonal, pyramidal. .... **Tetraedron regulare**
Cells (including the short spines) 14–45μm in diameter. Each cell has four angles caped with a short, blunt spine. One to many chromatophores, with or without pyrenoids. Common. (Plate XXXII.7).

    (b)   Cells pentagonal. .... **Tetraedron caudatum** (see 174)

  (iii)(a)   Cells triangular .... **Tetraedron muticum**
Cells 8.5–15μm long and 5–8μm thick, triangular in shape with rounded angles. Sides slightly concave. One to many chromatophores with or without pyrenoids. Common. (Plate XXXII.8).

    (b)   Cells quadrangular .... **Tetraedron minimum**
Cells 8–20μm long, 5–8μm thick, angles rounded and sides concave. Common. (Plate XXXII.9).

181. (b)   Cells elongate, crescent, or cigar-shaped **182**

182. (a)   Cells epiphytic on other algae .... **Characium**
Cells of **Characium** are ovoid to cylindrical or fusiform in shape, usually with a short stalk extending to a slightly swollen basal disc. Single chloroplast with one or more pyrenoids. Cells 15–70μm long, 2.5–33μm broad. Very common. The most frequent British species are **C.ambiguum**, **C.pringsheimii** and **C.seiboldii**. (Plate XXXII.10).

    (b)   Cells not epiphytic or attached **183**

183. (a)   Cells with single chloroplast filling most of the cell, usually with or without a pyrenoid. Cells needle like or fusiform **184**

    (b)   Cells with two axial chloroplasts, one in each half of the cell, each one with one or several pyrenoids arranged in a row **187**

184. (a)   Cells lunate to arcuate often in aggregates of 4–8–16 .... **Selenastrum**
The cells of **Selenastrum** are strongly curved and often occur in aggregations but without a mucilaginous surround. Single chromatophore filling the entire cell. Cells 2–8μm broad, 738μm long. Frequent in plankton. Chlorophyceae. **Selenastrum** is regarded by some authors as part of **Ankistrodesmus** (Plate XXXII.11).

115

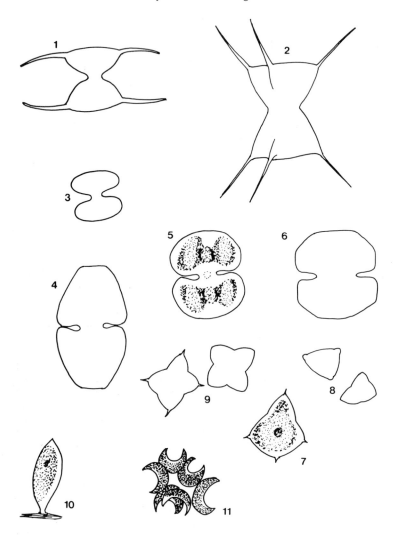

Plate XXXII. 1. Staurdesmus subulatus. 2. S.jaculiferous. 3. Cosmarium bioculatum. 4. Cosmarium pyramidatum. 5. C.prae-morsum. 6. C.rectangulare. 7. Tetraaedron regulare. 8. T.muticum. 9. T.minimum. 10. Characium. 11. Selenastrum.

184. (b)   Cells ovicular to fusiform, straight, curved or sigmoid occasionally in loose aggregations. **185**

185. (a)   Cells fusiform with ends drawn into long narrow spines, one of the spines is forked at end. .... **Ankyra**
Cells of **Ankyra** are spindle-shaped with long drawn out apices. Single chloroplast, 1 – several pyrenoids. Common in the plankton of lakes. Cells 70–90μm long, 4–5μm broad at centre. (Plate XXXIII.1). **Ankyra** closely resembles **Schroederia** except that the latter does not have a forked spine Both species resemble **Ankistrodesmus** and **Monoraphidium** but are slightly more robust. Chlorophyceae.

(b)   Cells do not have one spine forked and are not markedly fusiform **186**

186. (a)   Cells needle shaped, solitary .... **Monoraphidium**
Cells of **Monoraphidium** are needle shaped or sickle shaped but do not form colonies. Single chloroplast which almost fills cell sometimes with a pyrenoid. Abundant in eutrophic lakes. (Plate XXXIII.2).

(b)   Cells needle shaped occurring in irregular bundles or tangled groups .... **Ankistrodesmus**
Cells of **Ankistrodesmus** are very similar to those .of **Monoraphidium** except they occur in groups. An extremely common and often abundant species in eutrophic waters. (Plate XXXIII.3).

187. (a)   Cells straight with rounded or truncated poles. .. **Penium**
Cells of **Penium** are up to ten times as long as broad, and are cylindrical in shape. The cell apices are broadly rounded or truncate. A small median constriction may be present. Cell wall smooth or sometimes punctate. One chloroplast in each semicell, each with one to several pyrenoids. Cells 7–26μm broad, 10–274μm long. Common. (Plate XXXIII.4). Chlorophyceae.

(b)   Cells usually slightly or strongly curved with attenuated poles .... **Closterium**
Cells of **Closterium** are sickle shaped or even bow shaped. They may be fusiform or of relatively even width apart from the apices. Two chloroplasts (clearly ridged in larger species) each with several pyrenoids. A small vacuole is usually present at the apex of each chloroplast In these are often small granules (crystalline in structure) which show Brownian movement. Cell walls may be coloured by iron staining. Widespread (oligotrophic to eutrophic) and often abundant. They occur in all waters from lakes to farmyard pools. Chlorophyceae.

117

Detailed identification requires specialist texts but some of the more frequent species are indicated below.

(i)(a)   Cells strongly curved, 96–120μm long, 8–14μm broad, 3–6 pyrenoids .... **Closterium parvulum**
Cells strongly curved. Cell wall smooth. Chloroplasts with 7–8 ridges, terminal vacuoles with a number of moving granules. Common and widely distributed. (Plate XXXIII.5).

(b)   Cells only moderately or hardly curved .... **(ii)**

(ii)(a)   Cells very elongate and narrow, hardly curved, 440–590μm long, only 5–7μm broad. ..... **Closterium aciculare**
Cells are characteristically very long and narrow. Frequent in the plankton.
(Plate XXXIII.6).

(b)   Cells not as narrow .... **(iii)**

(iii)(a)   Cells moderately curved, concave margin with swollen region towards the centre, 220–370μm long, 35–50μm broad .... **Closterium moniliferum**
Common and widely distributed. Cells fairly broad in relation to their width and with more rounded apices. Inner margin of curve of cell swollen near centre. Chloroplasts with about 6 ridges and 6–7 pyrenoids each. Terminal vacuoles with moving granules. (Plate XXXIII.7).

(b)   Cell moderately curved, without swollen central area but with striations on the cell wall, 650–790μm long, 58–75μm broad .... **Closterium turgidum**
A large and typical species but not very common. The cell wall bears fine striations. Median girdle may be observed. Apices recurved. Chloroplasts with 7–8 ridges and 7–10 pyrenoids each. Terminal vacuoles with moving granules. (Plate XXXIII.8).

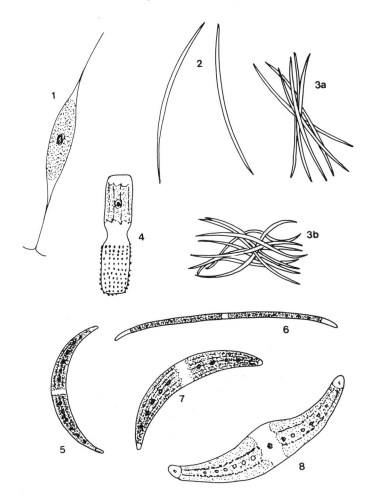

Plate XXXIII. 1. Ankyra. 2. Monoraphidium. 3. Ankistrodesmus. 4. Penium. 5. Closterium parvulum. 6. C.aciculare. 7. C.moniliferum. 8. C.turgidum

5. GLOSSARY OF TERMS

ACICULAR: needle shaped.

ACUMINATE: tapering gradually towards the apex.

ALTERNATING SERIES: a group of cells arranged side by side but with every other cell displaced either up or down relative to the mid-line (compare linear series).

ARCUATE: bow-shaped, strongly curved.

AREOLAE: forming a mosaic pattern.

ATTENUATE: narrowing to a point.

AUXOSPORE: resting spore produced by some diatoms.

AXIAL AREA: clear area of a diatom valve usually containing the raphe.

BENTHOS: living on bottom, on sediment surface.

BISERIATE: double row of cells.

BLOOM: a dense growth of algae which visibly discolours the water.

BRANCHING (True):   along the length of a filament one cell gives rise to two or more cells, one of which continues the main axis, the others growing off at an angle.

(False):   side growths occur along a filament but are formed by another portion of the filament growing sideways and not by a single cell giving rise to two or more others which themselves form branches.

BULBOUS: bulb-like, swollen at one end.

CALYPTRA: a hood or cap-like covering usually appearing on the apical cells of filaments.

CAPITATE: with a head, swollen at one or sometimes both ends.

CARINAL DOTS: circular or rod-shaped, evenly spaced dots along the keel edge of certain diatoms.

CENTRAL NODULE: A thickening on the inner face of the wall of some diatoms.

CENTRALES: diatoms which are radially symmetrical (centric diatoms).

CHLOROPLAST: an organelle within the cell containing the photosynthetic pigments.

CLATHRATE: with spaces between the cells.

CLAVATE: club-shaped.

COCCOID: rounded or spherical.

COENOBIUM: a colony of cells whose number is practically constant (often a multiple of four), this number being determined early on in its development. No further increase takes place until a new generation arises. The cells are arranged in a specific way.

COLLAR: a narrow neck around a flagellum opening in a shell or lorica.

COLONY: a group of individual cells joined together more or less permanently, or enclosed within the same sheath or matrix.

CONTRACTILE VACUOLE: small spherical body which regularly contracts, associated with osmoregulation, often found in flagellates.

COSTAE: ribs.

CRENULATE: finely wavy.

CRESCENT: an arc of a circle, a curved shape tapering at the ends.

CRESTED: the valve face in some diatoms is triangular or gable (as in a house) shaped in transverse section.

CUNEATE: wedge-shaped.

CYST: a thick walled resting spore whose walls may be impregnated with silica.

CYTOPLASM: all of the protoplasmic content of the cell, excluding the nucleus.

DAUGHTER CELLS: cells formed by division of mother cell.

DENDROID: tree-like, branching as in a tree. This refers to the colony shape in **Dinobryon**, which is not truly filamentous.

DICHOTOMOUS: forming two equal sized branches.

ELLIPSOIDAL: a figure with curved margins but elongate with the poles sharply rounded.

EPICONE: the upper or anterior half of a dinoflagellate cell.

EPILITHIC: growing on rocks.

EPIPHYTIC: growing on plants.

EXOSPORE: cyanobacterial spore produced by budding.

EPITHECA: the part of the cell wall of a dinoflagellate above the transverse furrow.

EYE-SPOT: a complex of granules, usually red or brown, sensitive to light, found in some motile algae.

FALSE BRANCHING: branching formed by another portion of a filament growing sideways and not by a single cell giving rise to two or more others which themselves form branches.

FILAMENT: a thread of cells arranged in a linear series. The cells are stacked end upon end. The series may be branched or unbranched.

FLAGELLUM: a whip-like organ of locomotion.

FLASK-LIKE: broad at the base and abruptly narrowing to a neck.

FRUSTULE: the shell of diatoms.

FUSIFORM: an elongate figure broadest at the centre and tapering at each end (spindle-shaped).

GAS VACUOLES: a protein covered gas filed organelle found in cyanobacteria.

GENUFLEXED: crooked, bent at an angle similar to a person bowing at the knee.

GIBBOUS: swollen to form a small locally occurring bump.

GIRDLE-VIEW: see definition of valves.

GLAUCOUS: greyish-green or green with a whitish overcast.

GLYCOGEN: a whitish carbohydrate similar to starch, a food reserve.

GONIDIA: spore-like thick walled reproductive cells in blue-green algae.

GRANULOSE: possessing granules.

GULLET: an opening through the membrane towards the anterior end of some flagellates.

HETEROCYST: an enlarged cell present in some filamentous blue-green algae, with thickened walls and often highly refractive, distinct from other cells. Concerned with nitrogen fixation.

HETEROPOLAR: where the ends (poles) of a diatom cell are of different shapes.

HETEROVALVAR: where each valve of a diatom cell is of a different shape.

H-PIECES: these are sections of cell walls. Some cell walls are composed of two overlapping halves which appear to be H-shaped. They are more conspicuous on the terminal cells of filaments when broken.

HYALINE: transparent, colourless.

HYPOCONE: the lower part of posterior half of a dinoflagellate cell.

HYPOTHECA:	the lower half of the cell wall of a dinoflagellate below the median girdle.
INTERCALARY:	arranged amongst the cells of a filament.
IODINE TEST:	the application of weak iodine solution to starch produces a blue-black colour. Even in algae producing starch this test may not always be obvious, as it depends upon the physiological state of the cell.
ISOBILATERAL:	each side of the cell, as divided by the longitudinal axis, the same shape.
ISOPOLAR:	both ends (poles) the same shape.
ISTHMUS:	the narrow part of a desmid cell connecting the two semicells.
KEEL:	a flange on the valve of some diatoms.
L.A.B:	long as broad – used in the key to compare length and breadth dimensions.
LAMELLATE:	composed of layers (see also laminate).
LANCEOLATE:	lance-shaped, long and narrow, with almost parallel margins but tapering towards the apex.
LEUCOSIN:	a whitish food reserve characteristic of many chrysophytes, usually found as highly refractive, rounded lumps.
LINEAR SERIES:	a series or row of cells arranged side by side in a straight line. (see for comparison alternating series).
LORICA:	a shell-like structure in which the organism lies. The shape varies but there is always an opening at one end, sometimes with a collar through which a flagellum passes.
LUNATE:	crescent or moon-shaped.
MATRIX:	surrounding matter, especially mucilage.
METABOLIC:	able to change its shape, cell wall not rigid (as in **Euglena**).
MICROMETRE:	μm: one thousandth of one millimetre.
MOTHER-CELL:	cells which divide to form daughter cells.
MULTISERIATE:	composed of many rows.
NANNOPLANKTON:	algae whose cell size is small enough to pass through a phytoplankton net.
OBOVOID:	with the broader end anterior, inversely ovoid.
OVATE:	a figure with elongate convex margins and broadly curved ends.
OVOID:	egg-shaped, the narrow end being anterior.
PARAMYLON:	a solid carbohydrate food reserve in some euglenoids.
PARIETAL:	arranged around the wall.

PELLICLE:	a thin membrane or sheet covering a cell.
PENNATE:	diatoms which are bilaterally symmetrical.
PERFORATION:	with holes or spaces especially between cells.
PERIPLAST:	the cell membrane of euglenoids, or other bounding membrane.
PHYCOCYANIN:	the blue-green pigments in the cells of cyanobacteria.
POLAR NODULE:	a body on the inner wall at the end of some diatoms and other algae.
POLAR SEPTUM:	a partition or cross-wall near the cell end.
PROSTRATE:	creeping along a substratum.
PSEUDOCILIUM:	flagellum like structure, but not an organ of locomotion, found in the **Tetrasporales**.
PSEUDORAPHE:	a false raphe, a clear area in the middle of the valves of some diatoms which forms a line resembling a true raphe but is not actually a canal.
PSEUDOVACUOLE:	a false vacuole. A pocket of gas or mucilage in the cytoplasm which is often refractive and resembles a true vacuole.
PUNCTATE:	bearing small pores or dots in the cell wall.
PYRENOID:	a protein body in the cell which may or may not have a starch sheath, usually buried in the chromatophore. If surrounded by starch, will stain darkly with iodine.
QUADRATE:	square or rectangular in shape.
RAPHE:	a longitudinal canal within the wall of some diatoms.
RENIFORM:	kidney-/or bean-shaped.
RETICULATE:	net-like.
RHOMBOID:	a parallelogram with oblique angles and adjacent sides unequal.
RIBBON:	large numbers of elongate cells joined by their sides to form a filament-like structure. In transverse section, however, a ribbon is never circular (e.g. **Fragilaria**). (see also strand).
ROSTRATE:	with a beak.
SCALARIFORM:	ladder like.
SEMICELL:	half a desmid cell.
SEPTUM:	a cross-partition either completely or partly across a cell.
SETA:	a hair arising from within a cell or a hair-like extension of a cell.
SETIFEROUS:	bearing setae or hairs.
SHEATH:	a covering envelope, often thin.

SIGMOID:	shaped like an S.
SILICEOUS WALL:	the wall of diatoms (and some other algae) is impregnated with silica. This often bears characteristic markings. Its presence can be detected by cold digestion in a strongly oxidizing acid to remove organic matter. If the cell wall withstands this treatment it is probably silica.
SINUS:	the deep furrow between the semicells of a desmid.
SIPHONACEOUS:	a tubular or filamentous-like thallus which has no cross-walls, e.g. **Vaucheria**.
STELLATE:	star-like.
STRAND:	see ribbon.
STRIAE:	delicate, sometimes long, narrow markings or lines.
SUB-RENIFORM:	nearly or almost reniform.
SULCUS:	a furrow or pair of furrows which may be found in the girdle area of some centric diatoms (e.g. **Melosira**).
TEST:	a rigid urn or post shaped surround to a cell (see also theca).
THALLUS:	a plant body with little differentiation of cells into tissues.
THECA:	see test.
TRANSAPICAL:	at right angles to the apical or long axis in diatoms.
TRICHOME:	a thread-like series of cells, exclusive of sheath, found in the blue-green algae.
TRUNCATE:	flat at the top.
UNDULATE:	wavy.
UNIAXIAL:	with a single main axis.
UNILATERAL:	arising from one side only.
UNISERIATE:	a single row of cells.
VACUOLES:	a space in the cytoplasm filed with cell sap and occasionally with granules.
VALVE:	one of two halves of a diatom cell wall. The valve view of the cell is seen from the top or the bottom and shows no overlapping portions. The girdle view is seen when the cell is viewed from the side and shows the overlapping of the two halves or valves.
VERRUCOSE:	warty.
WATER BLOOM:	a dense growth of planktonic algae which distinctly colours the water or forms a scum on the surface.

A Key to Common Algae

WHORLS:	several branches arising at same point around an axis.
XANTHOPHYLL:	a yellow pigment associated with chlorophyll.
ZOOSPORE:	a motile sexual spore.
ZOOSPORANGIUM:	cell producing zoospores.
ZYGOSPORE:	a thick walled resting spore formed by the fusion of two gametes.

6. REFERENCES

1. Fritsch, F.E. 1956. The structure and reproduction of the algae, Vol. 1. Cambridge University Press. 791pp.
2. Lee, R.E. 1980. Phycology. Cambridge University Press. 478pp.
3. Round, F.E. 1981. The ecology of the algae. Cambridge University Press. 653pp.
4. Christensen, T. 1962. Botanik. Systematisk Botanik, Vol II, No.2. Alger. Munksgaard, Kobanhavn.
5. Hendey, N.I. 1964. An introductory account of the smaller algae of British Coastal Waters. Part V. Bacillariophyceae (diatoms). Her Majesty's Stationary Office, London, UK. 397pp.
6. Barber, H.G. & Haworth, E.Y. 1981. A guide to the morphology of the diatom frustule. Freshwater Biological Association, U.K. Scientific Publication No. 44. F.B.A. The Ferry House, Ambleside, Cumbria LA22 OLP UK.
7. Round, F.E., Crawford, R.M. & Mann D.G. 1990. The diatoms. Biology and morphology of the genera. Cambridge University Press. 747pp.
8. Fogg, G.E. 1975. Algal cultures and phytoplankton ecology 2nd edition. University of London, London. 126pp.
9. Morris, I. 1967. An introduction to the algae. Hutchinson & Co.Ltd. London. 246pp.
10. Stewart, W.D.P. (Editor) 1974. Algal physiology and biochemistry. Botanical Monographs 10. Blackwell Scientific Publication.
11. Lund, J.W.G. 1945. Observations on soil algae. I. The ecology, size and taxonomy of British soil diatoms. New Phytologist, 44, 196.
12. Hartley, B. 1986. A check-list of the freshwater, brackish and marine diatoms of the British Isles and adjoining coastal waters. J. Mar. Biol. Ass. UK., 66, 531–610.
13. Round, F.E. 1981. The diatom genus Stephanodiscus. An electron-microscopic view of the classical species. Arch. Protistenk., 124, 455–470.

7. SELECTED BIBLIOGRAPHY FOR ADDITIONAL USE

Bourelly, P. 1966. Les Algues D'Eau Douce. Tome 1: Les Algues vertes.
Editions N. Boubee & Cie. Paris.
Bourelly, P. 1968. Les Algues D'Eau Douce. Tome 2: Les Algues
jaunes et brunes. Chrysophycees, Pheophycees, Xanthophycees et
Diatomees.
Editions N. Boubee & Cie. Paris.
Bourelly, P. 1970. Les Algues D'Eau Douce. Tome 3: Les Algues
bleues et rouges. Les Eugleniens Peridiniens et Cryptomonadines.
Editions N. Boubee & Cie. Paris.
Brook, A.J. 1981. The Biology of Desmids.
Blackwell, London.
Carr, N.G. & Whiton, B.A. (Eds) 1982. The Biology of Cyanobacteria.
Blackwell, London.
Desikachary, T.V. 1959. Cyanophyta.
Indian Council of (agricultural research. New Delhi.
Fritsch, F.E. 1956. The Structure and Reproduction of the Algae I and II.
Cambridge University Press.
Hustedt, F. 1930. Bacillariophyta (Diatomeae) Heft 10.
In A. Pascher: Die Susswasser-Flora Mitteleuropas.
Gustav Fischer, Jena.
Leedale, G.F. 1967. Euglenoid Flagellates.
Prentice-Hall Biological Science series.
Englewood Cliffs, N.J.
Lewin, R.A. (Editor) 1962. Physiology and Biochemistry of Algae.
Academic Press, U.S.A. (see Ref. 10 for an additional recent
review).
Lind, E.M. & Brook, A.J. 1980. Desmids of the English Lake District.
Freshwater Biological Association, U.K.
Scientific Publication No. 42. FBA, The Ferry House, Ambleside,
Cumbria, LA22 OLP, UK.
Pascher, A. 1913–36. Die Susswasserflora Deutschlands.
Oesterreichs und der Schweiz 15 vol.
Gustav Fischer, Jena.
Patrick, R. & Reimer, C.W. 1966, 1975. The Diatoms in the United
States 2 vol.
Monographs of the Academy of Natural Sciences, Philadelphia.
Prescott, G.W. 1951. Algae of the Western Great Lakes Area.
Wm. C. Brown, Dubuque, Iowa.
Reprint edition (1982) by Otto Koeltz Science Publishers, P.O.
Box 1380, D-6240 Koenigstein, F.R.G.

Reynolds, C.S. 1984. The Ecology of the Freshwater Phytoplankton.
    Cambridge University Press.
Smith, G.M. 1950. Freshwater Algae of the United States.
    McGraw Hill.
Werner, D. (Ed) 1977. The Biology of Diatoms.
    Blackwell, London, 498pp.
West, G.S. & Fritsch, F.E. 1927. A treatise on the British Freshwater
    Algae.
    Cambridge University Press.
West, W. & West, G.S. 1904. A Monograph of the British Desmidiaceae,
    Vols I to III.
    The Ray Society, London.

8. INDEX AND SPECIES LIST

A Key to Common Algae

Aulacoseira italica	26(a)	III.9
Auliscus	129(a)	XX.9
Batrachospermum	11(a)	I.4
Biddulphia	136(a)	XXII.4
Botryococcus braunii	82(a)	XIII.7
Bulbochaetae	15(b)	II.4
Caloneis amphisbaena	166(a)	XXIX.1
Carteria	112(b)	XVIII.5
Ceratium hirundinella	119(a)	XIX.7
Chaetoceros	135(a)	XXII.3
Chaetopeltis	91(b)	XV.2
Chaetophora	16(b)	II.5
Chamaesiphon confervicola	55(a)	X.6
Chamaesiphon incrustans	55(a)	X.5
Chara	2(a)	I.1
Characium ambiguum	182(a)	XXXII.10
Characium pringsheimii	182(a)	
Characium seiboldii	182(a)	
Chlamydomonas angulosa	118(b)	XIX.5
Chlamydomonas globosa	118(b)	XIX.6
Chlamydomonas plalyrhyncha	118(b)	XIX.3
Chlamydomonas sphagnicola	118(b)	XIX.4
Chlorella pyrenoidosa	172(a)	XXX.4
Chlorella vulgaris	172(a)	XXX.5
Chodatella	171(b)	XXX.3
Chromulina	109(b)	XVIII.2
Chroococcus limneticus	61(b)	XI.5
Chroococcus turgidus	61(b)	XI.6
Chroomonas	116(a)	XVIII.8
Cladophora glomerata	23(b)	III.3
Cladophora sauteri	23(b)	III.3
Closterium aciculare	187(b)	XXXIII.6
Closterium moniliferum	187(b)	XXXIII.7
Closterium parvulum	187(b)	XXXIII.5
Closterium turgidum	187(b)	XXXIII.8
Cocconeis pediculus	139(a)	XXII.7
Cocconeis placentula	139(a)	XXII.8
Cocconeis scutullum	139(a)	XXII.6
Coelastrum cambricum	94(b)	XV.5b
Coelastrum microporum	94(b)	XV.5a
Coelosphaerium keutzingianum	58(b)	X.12
Coelosphaerium naegelianum	58(b)	X.13
Coleochaetae	12(b)	II.2

Coscinodiscus lacustris	132(b)	XXI.8
Cosmarium biocalatum	179(b)	XXXII.3
Cosmarium praemorsum	179(b)	XXXII.5
Cosmarium pyramidatum	179(b)	XXXII.4
Cosmarium rectagulare	179(b)	XXXII.6
Crucigenia rectangularis	101(b)	
Crucigenia tetrapedia	101(b)	XVI.8
Cryptomonas erosa	116(b)	XVIII.10
Cryptomonas ovata	116(b)	XVIII.9
Cryptomonas tetrapyrenoidosa	116(b)	XVIII.11
Cyclotella compta	131(a)	XXI.6
Cyclotella glomerata	131(a)	XXI.3
Cyclotella kutzingiana	131(a)	XXI.5
Cyclotella meneghiniana	131(a)	XXI.4
Cyclotella operculata	131(a)	XXI.2
Cylindrospermum majus	48(a)	VIII.3
Cylindrospermum stagnale	48(a)	VIII.3
Cymatopleura elliptica	150(a)	XXV.7
Cymatopleura solea	150(a)	XXV.6
Cymbella cistula	148(b)	XXV.1
Cymbella cuspidata	148(b)	XXIV.10
Cymbella gracilis	148(b)	XXV.4
Cymbella lanceolata	148(b)	XXV.2
Cymbella minuta	148(b)	XXIV.9
Cymbella sinuata	148(b)	XXIV.8
Cymbella turgida	148(b)	XXV.3
Desmidium aptogonum	32(b)	VI.2
Desmidium swartzii	32(b)	VI.2
Diatoma elongatum	28(b)	V.1
Diatoma hiemale	28(b)	V.2
Diatoma vulgare	28(b)	V.3
Dictyosphaerium ehrenbergianum	81(a)	XIII.6
Dictyosphaerium pulchellum	81(a)	XIII.6
Didymosphenia	156(a)	XXVI.8
Dinobryon	7(a)	I.6
Draparnaldia	17(a)	II.6
Dunaliella	118(b)	
Elakatothrix gelatinosa	80(b)	XIII.5
Enteromorpha intestinalis	34(a)	VI.4
Epithemia turgida	147(a)	XXIV.2
Epithemia zebra	147(a)	XXIV.3
Eudorina elegans	70(b)	XII.4
Eunotia arcus	145(a)	XXIII.8
Eunotia exigua	145(a)	XXIII.7

Eunotia pectinalis	145(a)	XXIII.9
Eunotia robusta	145(a)	XXIII.10
Fragilaria capucina	27(b)	IV.4
Fragilaria construens	27(b)	IV.2
Fragilaria crotonensis	27(b)	IV.1
Fragilaria pinnata	27(b)	IV.3
Fragilaria virescens	27(b)	IV.5
Frustulia rhomboides	162(a)	XXVII.4
Frustulia vulgaris	162(a)	XXVIII.3
Geminella	30(a)	V.9
Glenodinium	121(b)	XIX.12
Gloeocapsa alpina	61(a)	XI.3
Gloeocapsa rupestris	61(a)	XI.2
Gloeocapsa turgida	61(a)	XI.1
Gloeocystis gigas	85(b)	XIII.10a
Gloeocystis vesiculosa	85(b)	XIII.10b
Gloeotrichia natans	47(a)	VIII.1
Gloeotrichia pisum	47(a)	VIII.1
Golenkinia radiata	170(a)	XXX.1
Gomphonema constrictum	156(b)	XXVI.9
Gomphonema olivaceum	156(b)	XXVI.11
Gomphonema parvulum	156(b)	XXVI.10
Gomphosphaeria aponia	58(a)	X.10
Gomphosphaeria lacustris	58(a)	X.11
Gongrosira	20(b)	II.8
Gonium sociale	70(a)	
Gonium pectorale	70(a)	XII.3
Gymnodinium	121(a)	XIX.11
Gyrosigma attenuatum	142(a)	XXIII.4
Gyrosigma spencerii	142(a)	XXIII.5
Haematococcus lacustris	117(a)	XIX.1
Hantzschia amphioxys	152(a)	XXV.8
Hildenbrandia	12(a)	II.1
Hormidium	41(b)	VII.7
Hyalodiscus	130(a)	XXI.1
Hydrodictyon reticulatum	6(a)	I.3
Kirchneriella lunaris	80(a)	XIII.4a
Kirchneriella obesa	80(a)	XIII.4b
Lagerheimia quadriseta	170(a)	XXX.2

Nitzschia frustulum	152(b)	XXVI.4
Nitzschia hungarica	152(b)	XXVI.2
Nitzschia linearis	152(b)	XXVI.1
Nitzschia palea	152(b)	XXVI.5
Nitzschia sigma	152(b)	XXV.11
Nitzschia sigmoidea	152(b)	XXV.12
Nitzschia triblionella	152(b)	XXV.10
Nostoc coeruleum	50(b)	IX.1
Nostoc commune	50(b)	IX.5
Nostoc verrucosum	50(b)	IX.3
Nostoc piscinale	50(b)	IX.2
Nostoc pruniforme	50(b)	IX.4
Oedogonium	39(b)	VI.8
Oocystis crassa	172(b)	XXX.6
Oocystis elliptica	172(b)	XXX.11
Oocystis gigas	172(b)	XXX.9
Oocystis natans	172(b)	XXX.10
Oocystis parva	172(b)	XXX.8
Oocystis solitaria	172(b)	XXX.7
Oscillatoria agardhii	52(a)	IX.12
Oscillatoria brevis	52(a)	IX.14
Oscillatoria limnetica	52(a)	IX.9
Oscillatoria limosa	52(a)	IX.8
Oscillatoria princeps	52(a)	IX.7
Oscillatoria redekii	52(a)	IX.10
Oscillatoria rubescens	52(a)	IX.11
Oscillatoria tenvis	52(a)	IX.13
Palmella	86(a)	XIV.1
Pandorina morum	68(a)	XII.1
Pediastrum boryanum	89(a)	XIV.7
Pediastrum clathratum	89(a)	XIV.3
Pediastrum duplex	89(a)	XIV.4
Pediastrum simplex	89(a)	XIV.5
Pediastrum tetras	89(a)	XIV.6
Penium	187(a)	XXXIII.4
Peridinium cinctum	120(b)	XIX.10
Peridinium inconspicuum	120(b)	XIX.8
Peridinium willei	120(b)	XIX.9
Peronia	155(a)	XXVI.7
Phacus caudatus	107(a)	XVII.2
Phacus longicauda	107(a)	XVII.1
Phacus pleuronectes	107(a)	XVII.3
Phormidium autumnale	53(b)	X.3

Phormidium tenue	53(b)	X.4
Pinnularia alpina	161(a)	XXVIII.2
Pinnularia viridis	161(a)	XXVIII.1
Pleurococcus	101(a)	XVI.7
Pleurosigma aestuarii	142(b)	XXIII.6
Pleurosigma strigosum	142(b)	XXIII.6
Pleurotaenium	176(a)	XXXI.1
Protoderma viride	90(b)	XV.1
Pteromonas angulosa	118(a)	XIX.2
Pyramimonas	112(a)	XVIII.4
Rhizoclonium hieroglyphium	23(a)	III.2
Rhizosolenia eriensis	134(a)	XXII.1
Rhodomonas minuta	115(a)	XVIII.7
Rhoicosphenia curvata	146(a)	XXIV.1
Rivularia haematites	47(b)	VIII.2
Rivularia minutula	47(b)	VIII.2
Scenedesmus abundans	97(a)	XVI.5
Scenedesmus acuminatus	97(a)	XV.10
Scenedesmus acutus	97(a)	XV.8
Scenedesmus arcuatus	97(a)	XV.7
Scenedesmus armatus	97(a)	XVI.2
Scenedesmus denticulatus	97(a)	XVI.3
Scenedesmus dimorphus	97(a)	XVI.1
Scenedesmus obliquus	97(a)	XV.9
Scenedesmus quadricauda	97(a)	XVI.4
Scytonema alatum	44(a)	VII.8
Scytonema mirabile	44(a)	VII.8
Selenastrum	184(a)	XXXII.11
Sorastrum	95(a)	XV.6
Spermatozopsis exsultans	111(a)	XVIII.3
Sphaerella	117(a)	XIX.1
Sphaerocystis	86(b)	XIV.2
Spirogyra (condensata group)	29(a)	V.5
Spirogyra (Crassa group)	29(a)	V.6
Spirogyra (Inflata group)	29(a)	V.7
Spirogyra (Insignis group)	29(s)	V.8
Spirulina major	51(a)	IX.6
Spirulina platensis	51(a)	IX.6
Spirulina subsalsa	51(a)	IX.6
Spondylosium papilosum	32(a)	VI.1
Spondylosium planum	32(a)	VI.1
Staurastrum anatinum	178(a)	XXXI.8
Staurastrum cingulum	178(a)	XXXI.10

Tribonema bombycinum	40(b)	VII.4
Tribonema minus	40(b)	VII.2
Tribonema viride	40(b)	VII.3
Triceratium	137(a)	XXII.5
Ulothrix aequalis	41(a)	VII.6
Ulothrix zonata	41(a)	VII.5
Uroglena	71(a)	XII.5
Urosolenia	134(a)	XXII.1
Vaucheria	8(a)	I.7
Volvox tertius	71(b)	XII.6
Volvox aureus	71(b)	XII.7
Volvox globator	71(b)	XII.8
Westella	94(a)	XV.4
Zygnema	35(a)	VI.5